Nita Mehta's™
COOKING

Nita Mehta
B.Sc. (Home Science) M.Sc. (Food and Nutrition) Gold Medalist

co author:
ANU KSHETRAPAL

Snab Publishers Pvt Ltd

Corporate Office
3A/3, Asaf Ali Road, New Delhi 110 002
Phone: +91 11 2325 2948, 2325 0091
Telefax: +91 11 2325 0091
E-mail: nitamehta@nitamehta.com
Website: www.nitamehta.com

Editorial and Marketing office
E-159, Greater Kailash II, New Delhi 110 048

Food Styling and Photography by Snab
Typesetting by National Information Technology Academy
3A/3, Asaf Ali Road, New Delhi 110 002

Recipe Development & Testing:
Nita Mehta Foods - R & D Centre
3A/3, Asaf Ali Road, New Delhi - 110002

Distributed by :
NITA MEHTA BOOKS
3A/3, Asaf Ali Road, New Delhi - 02
Distribution Centre :
D16/1, Okhla Industrial Area, Phase-I,
New Delhi - 110020
Tel.: 26813199, 26813200
E-mail: nitamehta.mehta@gmail.com

Contributing Writers :
Anurag Mehta
Tanya Mehta
Subhash Mehta
Editors :
Sangeeta
Sunita

© Copyright Snab Publishers Pvt Ltd 2014
All rights reserved

ISBN 978-81-7869-002-5

First Print 2014

Cover Designed by: **SNAB**

Printed in India at Infinity Advertising Services (P) Ltd, New Delhi

World rights reserved: The contents - all recipes, photographs and drawings are original and copyrighted. No portion of this book shall be reproduced, stored in a retrieval system or transmitted by any means, electronic, mechanical, photocopying, recording or otherwise, without the written permission of the publishers. While every precaution is taken in the preparation of this book, the publishers and the author assume no responsibility for errors or omissions. Neither is any liability assumed for damages resulting from the use of information contained herein.

TRADEMARKS ACKNOWLEDGED: Trademarks used, if any, are acknowledged as trademarks of their respective owners. These are used as reference only and no trademark infringement is intended upon. Ajinomoto (monosodium glutamate, MSG) is a trademark of Aji-no-moto company of Japan. Use it sparingly if you must as a flavour enhancer.

Price: Rs. 295/-

Introduction

With the world shrinking due to wide spread travelling, food habits have undergone a vast change. People today enjoy a wide variety of food from far and near. Continental meals are also becoming popular in addition to the growing popularity of the flavourful Indian curries, the world over.

Generally in Continental cooking, the sauce is cooked separately and so are the meat and the vegetables. The two are then combined at the time of serving. The sauce may be tomato based, cream based or just stock thickened with cornflour. Mustard, lemon, pepper, fresh or dried herbs are added to flavour the sauces.

This book offers you a wide variety of chicken, mutton, fish, egg, pasta and vegetable dishes to help you pick and choose a complete Continental meal. But keep in mind, not to make more than 2-3 oven or baked dishes, unless you have a large oven, to avoid last minute confusion. The book has been divided into sections which will be of great help in planning the menu. If you are preparing a baked fish or mutton, then make a pan roast chicken which does not require the oven; or vice versa. Make light sesame vegetables with pan roast chicken. Serve the food with a warm bread basket.

Enjoy Continental cooking with confidence!

Contents

Introduction 3

SOUPS 6

To Make Chicken Stock 6	Spring Onion & Potato Soup 9
Cream of Chicken Soup 7	French Onion Soup 10
Cream of Tomato Soup 8	Cream of Chicken & Mushroom Soup . 12

SALADS 13

Tomatoes Stuffed with Chicken Salad .. 14	Warm Winter Salad 20
Chicken Cole Slaw 15	Yogurt-Mayo Salad 21
Broccoli & Bean Salad 16	Russian Salad 22
Caesar Salad with Chicken 18	

FROM THE OVEN (BAKED & GRILLED) 24

Toppings for Baked Dishes 25	Onion-Mushroom Rosti 42
Accompaniments to Grills 25	Mushroom Pate 42
Rice, Spinach & Mushroom Casserole . 26	Pancake Florentine 44
Moussaka 27	Chicken Amandine 46
Baked Fish in Cheese Custard 28	Chicken Casserole 48
Cauliflower & Broccoli Bake 30	Baked Corn with Asparagus 49
Exotic Vegetables Au gratin 32	Hot Cheese Souffle 50
Grilled Fish with Tangy Sauce 34	Baked Tomato Fish 51
French Egg Casserole 36	Vegetable & Cheese Souffle 52
Lemon Fish Florentine 37	Corn & Spinach Souffle 52
Quiche Lorraine 38	Shepherd's Pie 54
Grilled Savoury Chicken 40	King Edward's Potatoes 55
Bean & Spinach Bake 41	Chicken Roast 56
	Chicken Alexandria 58

FROM THE PAN 59

Supreme Vegetable Steak 60	Hungarian Goulash 76
Mince Pattise & Mushroom Sauce........ 61	Chicken Stroganoff 78
Dill Potatoes 62	Chicken Italiano 80
Fried Chicken Chasseur 64	Velvety Prawns 81
Light Sesame Vegetables 64	Pan Fried Herb Chicken 82
Champignons Ala Cream.................... 66	Chickpeas with Paneer 83
Herbed Fish with Tartare Sauce 67	Crispy Fried Chicken 84
Vegetable Sizzler 68	Mince Crepes 85
Nutty Fish Balls in Tomato Sauce 70	Chicken with Mushroom Cream......... 86
Aubergines with Sour Cream 71	Black Pepper Lamb Chops................. 87
Chicken Sizzler 72	Chicken Breasts with Orange Glaze.... 88
Fettuccine with Chicken 74	Mexican Cheese Steaks 89
Vegetable Stew 75	Chicken Stew.................................... 90

BREADS 92

Flavoured Bread Spreads 92	Baked Bread Loaf 92

DESSERTS & PUDDINGS 93

Blueberry Cheese Cake 94	Creme Caramel.................................. 99
Devil's Chocolate Temptation 95	Lemon Souffle................................. 100
Prune & Walnut Pie 96	Meringue Rice Pudding.................... 101
Mocha Mousse 98	Almond Praline Souffle.................... 102

International Conversion Guide.........................104

Soups

Home made soups are highly nutritious and wonderfully versatile. A well flavoured stock forms the base of many soups, but if stock is not available you can use a stock cube (chicken or vegetable seasoning) mixed with water. 1 stock cube is generally mixed with 4 cups of water. Whenever you use a stock cube, remember that it already has salt, so add salt and other seasoning only after tasting the soup. In all the recipes, the cup used is an ordinary tea cup which holds about 200 ml of liquid

To Make Chicken Stock

Makes 4 cups

250 gm chicken (wings, back and 1 breast piece or 2 chicken breasts)
1 bay leaf (*tej patta*), 6 cups water

1. Pressure cook together chicken wings, neck, back, giblet with water and bay leaves (*tej patta*) to give 1-2 whistles.

2. Remove from fire and let the pressure drop by itself. Strain. Remove the meat from the pieces and keep aside. Add the bones to the liquid. Simmer the liquid on low heat for 15 minutes or even more. Use the liquid as the stock.

NOTE: If using chicken carcase (chicken with skin) for the stock, chill the prepared stock. A layer of fat will collect on the top. Skim the fat from the surface to get a clear stock.

A good stock always has a gelatine formation when cold.

If adding vegetables also with the chicken, use mild flavoured vegetables like carrots, leek, celery or potatoes as chicken has a delicate flavour. The strong flavoured vegetables like cauliflower, turnip, cabbage if used with chicken are inclined to predominate the chicken flavour.

Cream of Chicken Soup

Serves 4

200-250 gm chicken (wings, back and 1 breast piece or 2 chicken breasts)
1 bay leaf (*tej patta*), 4½ cups water
1 tbsp butter, 1½-2 tbsp flour (*maida*)
1¼ cups milk, 1 tsp salt, ¼ tsp pepper, or to taste

GARNISH

1 tbsp chopped parsley or coriander, 2 tbsp cream

1. Place the chicken pieces in a pressure cooker with a bay leaf and 4½ cups of water and pressure cook to give 1-2 whistles. Reduce heat and simmer for 15-20 minutes. Remove from heat and cool. Remove the meat from the bones.
2. Discard the bones and bay leaf. Mix chicken pieces (reserve a few pieces to garnish) with the stock (liquid). Blend the stock and chicken pieces in a mixer blender.
3. Strain the blended stock through a metal sieve to get a creamy mixture. (Discard the chicken meat residue).
4. Heat butter in a pan. Add flour and stir for 1 minute.
5. Add milk and stir till slightly thick and creamy.
6. Add the blended and strained chicken stock. Bring to a boil.
7. Add salt, pepper and chopped coriander or parsley.
8. Check the seasoning (salt & pepper) and serve hot garnished with a little cream.

Cream of Tomato Soup

Serves 8

1 kg (12 medium) red tomatoes
1 carrot - chopped, 1 onion - chopped, 1 potato - chopped
4-5 cloves (*laung*), 6-8 peppercorns (*saboot kali mirch*)
1" stick of cinnamon (*dalchini*)
2 tbsp butter
2 tsp salt, 1-2 tsp sugar
2 tbsp cornflour, a few drops of lemon juice

GARNISHING

4-5 tbsp cream
1 bread - cut into tiny cubes and stir fried in a little butter to make bread croutons
fresh parsley or coriander leaves - chopped

1. Heat 2 tbsp butter in a pressure cooker. Add onion, carrot, potato, cloves, peppercorns and cinnamon. Cook until onion turns pale and transparent.
2. Add washed whole tomatoes.
3. Add 6 cups water and pressure cook to give 2 whistles. Remove from fire.
4. Mash the tomatoes slightly and strain.
5. Churn the unstrained part in a mixer.
6. Strain again. Throw away the solid unstrained part in the sieve.
7. Keep the soup on fire. Boil, stirring occasionally.
8. Add 2 tbsp cornflour dissolved in ½ cup of water.
9. Add salt, pepper and sugar and cook for 5-7 minutes. Add lemon juice to taste.
10. Serve hot garnished with coriander leaves, few croutons and a swirl of cream.

NOTE: To make croutons, cut 1 day old bread into small cubes and saute in 1 tbsp melted butter in a pan till golden.

Spring Onion & Potato Soup

Serves 4-5

BOIL TOGETHER

1 spring onion - chopped upto the greens, 1 potato - chopped
8-10 peppercorns (*saboot kali mirch*), ½" piece ginger - chopped
1 tsp salt, or to taste, 4 cups water

OTHER INGREDIENTS

1 cup milk, ½ tsp butter, 2 tsp lemon juice (juice of ½ lemon)
2-3 almonds - roasted on a griddle (*tawa*) and very thinly sliced, for garnishing

1. Boil spring onion, potato, peppercorns, ginger, salt and water together in a pan. After the boil keep on low heat and cook covered, for about 15 minutes, till potatoes turn soft.
2. Remove from fire. Strain and keep the liquid aside. Cool. Blend the onions etc. to a puree with a little liquid.
3. Add the rest of the liquid and 1 cup milk to the puree. Keep on fire. Boil. Simmer on low heat for 5-7 minutes.
4. Add lemon juice and salt to taste. Add ½ tsp of butter if desired. Remove from fire. Serve hot garnished with greens of onion and some roasted and finely sliced almonds.

French Onion Soup

Serves 4

3 tbsp butter
2 onions - sliced very finely
4 flakes garlic - crushed
1½ tbsp flour (*maida*)
salt to taste
black pepper powder to taste
4 cups stock (given below) or water

STOCK
1 carrot - chopped roughly
1 onion - chopped roughly
2 bay leaves (*tej patta*)
6-7 peppercorns (*saboot kali mirch*)
4 cups water

GARNISHING
25 gm cheese - grated
½ tsp mustard powder
1 slice of bread or 4 slices of garlic loaf - toasted

1. To prepare the stock, pressure cook all ingredients of the stock with 4 cups water to give 3-4 whistles. Pass through a sieve. Keep stock aside.
2. Heat the butter in a clean, heavy bottomed pan. Fry the onions and garlic over a moderately low heat, stirring occasionally to prevent sticking, until brown. Do not let the onions burn.
3. Add the flour and cook for 1 minute on low flame. Pour in the stock gradually, stirring continuously. Boil. Season with salt and pepper, and simmer for 5 minutes. Keep soup aside.
4. To garnish the soup, mix the mustard powder and cheese together in a small bowl. Blend well. Spread over the toasted bread. Place the toasted slice in the oven for a few minutes. Cut into 4 squares if using normal bread.
5. Serve steaming hot soup with one piece of cheese toast floating on top in each serving.

NOTE: You could use a vegetarian seasoning or stock cube mixed with water instead of preparing a stock.

Cream of Chicken & Mushroom Soup

The mushrooms give the creamy texture and flavour to the chicken soup.

Serves 4-5

5½ cups chicken stock or water
1 cup milk
½ cup shredded chicken
75 gm mushrooms - roughly chopped
1½ tbsp butter
1½ tbsp plain flour (*maida*)
salt and pepper to taste
1 tbsp chopped parsley or coriander and 2 tbsp fresh cream, to garnish

1. Mix the chicken stock and milk and keep aside.
2. Heat butter in a pan.
3. Add mushrooms and fry for 4-5 minutes on low heat till soft.
4. Sprinkle the flour over the mushrooms and stir on low heat for ½ minute.
5. Add stock and milk mixture. Bring to a boil, stirring continuously till thick.
6. Add shredded chicken, salt and pepper. Cook for a minute.
7. Serve hot, garnished with fresh cream and parsley.

Salads

Salads are a combination of crisp fresh greens, fruits, boiled chicken, salami, sausages, corn, cheese etc. which are made more exotic and tasty with a dressing like vinaigrette, mayonnaise or whisked hung yogurt.

Tomatoes Stuffed with Chicken Salad

A delicious salad, looks beautiful when placed in the centre of the table.

Serves 8

8 medium tomatoes
1 chicken breast - boiled & shredded
2 canned pineapple slices - squeezed & cut into tiny pieces
2 tbsp shredded cabbage

THOUSAND ISLAND DRESSING

3 tbsp mayonnaise, 1 tbsp thick cream, 1 tbsp ready made tomato puree
a few drops of tabasco sauce
¼ tsp pepper, salt to taste
1 tsp finely chopped onion, 1 tsp finely chopped capsicum

1. Wash chicken. Pressure cook with ½ tsp salt and ½ cup water to give one whistle. Debone the meat and shred it into small pieces.
2. Wash and dry tomatoes. Cut a slice from the top and scoop out the pulp carefully.
3. Sprinkle salt and pepper inside the tomato. Keep them upside down.
4. Cut pineapple slices in small pieces. Squeeze gently to remove excess syrup.
5. Mix pineapple pieces, shredded chicken and cabbage in a bowl.
6. Mix together - mayonnaise, cream, tomato puree, Worcestershire sauce, salt and pepper to taste. Add chopped onion and capsicum also.
7. Pour the mayonnaise over the chicken. Mix. Fill the tomatoes with the mixture.
8. Decorate on a bed of salad leaves. Serve chilled.

NOTE: Boiled prawns can be used instead of chicken. Also coloured peppers can be roasted whole on a naked flame to char them slightly and turn soft. Scrape the blackened skin with a knife and cut each into two to get 2 cups from one bell pepper. Scoop out the seeds and fill with salad. Press lightly.

Salads

Salads are a combination of crisp fresh greens, fruits, boiled chicken, salami, sausages, corn, cheese etc. which are made more exotic and tasty with a dressing like vinaigrette, mayonnaise or whisked hung yogurt.

Tomatoes Stuffed with Chicken Salad

A delicious salad, looks beautiful when placed in the centre of the table.

Serves 8

8 medium tomatoes
1 chicken breast - boiled & shredded
2 canned pineapple slices - squeezed & cut into tiny pieces
2 tbsp shredded cabbage

THOUSAND ISLAND DRESSING

3 tbsp mayonnaise, 1 tbsp thick cream, 1 tbsp ready made tomato puree
a few drops of tabasco sauce
¼ tsp pepper, salt to taste
1 tsp finely chopped onion, 1 tsp finely chopped capsicum

1. Wash chicken. Pressure cook with ½ tsp salt and ½ cup water to give one whistle. Debone the meat and shred it into small pieces.
2. Wash and dry tomatoes. Cut a slice from the top and scoop out the pulp carefully.
3. Sprinkle salt and pepper inside the tomato. Keep them upside down.
4. Cut pineapple slices in small pieces. Squeeze gently to remove excess syrup.
5. Mix pineapple pieces, shredded chicken and cabbage in a bowl.
6. Mix together - mayonnaise, cream, tomato puree, Worcestershire sauce, salt and pepper to taste. Add chopped onion and capsicum also.
7. Pour the mayonnaise over the chicken. Mix. Fill the tomatoes with the mixture.
8. Decorate on a bed of salad leaves. Serve chilled.

NOTE: Boiled prawns can be used instead of chicken. Also coloured peppers can be roasted whole on a naked flame to char them slightly and turn soft. Scrape the blackened skin with a knife and cut each into two to get 2 cups from one bell pepper. Scoop out the seeds and fill with salad. Press lightly.

Chicken Cole Slaw

Serves 4-6

2 cups shredded cabbage
2 chicken breasts
1 small onion - chopped finely, 1 large carrot - grated
2-3 slices pineapple or 1 orange - skinned, peeled and cubed, a few black grapes
¾ cup mayonnaise
2 tbsp cream (optional)

VINAIGRETTE DRESSING
2 tbsp vinegar, 6-8 tbsp olive oil or any cooking oil
1 tsp mustard powder, ¼ tsp salt, ¼ tsp sugar, ¼ tsp pepper powder

1. Blend all the ingredients of the dressing together by shaking all together in a bottle.
2. Place the chicken breasts in a pressure cooker with ½ cup water and ¼ tsp salt. Pressure cook to give 1-2 whistles. Remove from heat. Cool and flake the chicken meat into small pieces.
3. Remove the hard core of the cabbage and shred very finely with a sharp knife or in a food processor.
4. Mix cabbage, onion and chicken in a salad bowl. Pour the vinaigrette dressing over and chill covered in the refrigerator for 4-5 hours.
5. After 4-5 hours, drain if any vinaigrette dressing is at the bottom of the bowl.
6. Add carrot, pineapple or orange and grapes to the salad bowl.
7. Pour mayonnaise and cream over and mix gently.
8. Taste the coleslaw for seasoning and add salt, pepper and mustard according to taste. Serve chilled.

Broccoli & Bean Salad

Serves 4

150 gm tender french beans - threaded & cut into 1½" long pieces
1 small broccoli - cut into medium florets
1-2 strawberries, optional

MUSTARD DRESSING
2 tsp mustard paste
2 tbsp extra virgin olive oil
½ tsp peppercorns - crushed
½ tsp salt
1 tbsp lemon juice
3-4 flakes garlic - sliced finely and crushed lightly

1. Mix all ingredients of the dressing together in a small bowl.
2. Boil 4-5 cups water with 2 tsp salt and 2 tsp sugar. Add beans to the boiling water.
3. As soon as the boil returns, keep the beans boiling for 1 minute. Add broccoli as soon as the boil returns, remove from fire and let veggies be in hot water for a minute. Strain veggies. Refresh by taking them out of cold water.
4. Leave in the strainer to drain out all the water. Pat dry the beans on a paper napkin and transfer them to a mixing bowl.
5. Add the dressing to the beans. Toss to mix well. Cover and refrigerate.
6. At the time of serving, mix in 1 tsp toasted sesame seeds. Transfer to a serving bowl and serve sprinkled with some more toasted sesame seeds.

Caesar Salad with Chicken

Serves 4

½ bunch lettuce leaves (50 gm)
2 chicken breasts, 2 hard boiled eggs
1 large tomato - deseeded & cut into thin long pieces

STIR FRIED GARLIC CROUTONS
2 slices white bread, 2 tsp butter
2-3 flakes garlic - crushed
4-6 peppercorns - crushed

GARNISH
2 tbsp parmesan cheese (optional)

DRESSING
6 tbsp olive oil, 2 tbsp vinegar or wine vinegar, 1 tbsp lemon juice
2 flakes garlic - crushed & chopped finely
¾ tsp salt, ¼ tsp black pepper powder, 1 tsp sugar
1 tsp mustard paste or powder

1. Place the chicken breasts in a pressure cooker with 1 cup water and ½ tsp salt. Pressure cook to give 1-2 whistles and then remove from heat. Cool. Coarsely chop the breast into small pieces. Put the chicken pieces in a small bowl.
2. Wash the lettuce and discard the outer hard leaves. Tear the tender leaves into small pieces. Soak in chilled water.
3. Mix all the ingredients of the dressing in a small bottle and shake well.
4. Pour the dressing over the chicken pieces in the bowl & mix well. Cover & refrigerate.
5. To make croutons, mix butter with garlic and peppercorns and spread on one side of the slice. Remove the sides of the bread and cut into small cubes. Cook them in an ungreased non stick pan over medium heat for 5-7 minutes, stirring frequently, till golden brown. Remove from pan and keep aside.
6. Hard boil eggs by boiling them for 8-10 minutes in water. Remove from hot water & immediately put in cold water to prevent the formation of a black ring around the yolk. Cool, shell & cut each egg into 4 slices lengthwise. Keep aside.
7. At serving time, roll the lettuce leaves in a clean kitchen towel to dry. Mix lettuce leaves, tomatoes, eggs and croutons in a large salad bowl. Pour the dressing along with the chicken pieces on the vegetables etc. Toss gently with a fork. Garnish with cheese. Serve at once.

Warm Winter Salad

Serves 4

100 gm (30-35) small, tender spinach leaves - dipped in ice cold water for 1-2 hours
100 gm button mushrooms, choose small ones
50 gm baby corns (3-4 pieces), 4-5 florets of broccoli - blanched
6-8 thick slices of zucchini - halved, 1 firm tomato or 3-4 cherry tomatoes, halved
3 tbsp olive oil or any cooking oil

DRESSING
1 tbsp lemon juice, 2 tbsp orange juice
4 tbsp any cooking oil
1 tsp honey, 2 flakes garlic - crushed and chopped
6-8 ginger juliennes, ¼ tsp salt and ¼ tsp pepper

GARNISH, OPTIONAL
1 tbsp roasted sesame seeds (*til*) - roasted

1. Prepare the dressing by mixing, lemon juice, orange juice, oil, garlic, salt and pepper. with a whisk till it turns thick. Keep aside.
2. Remove the stems of spinach leaves. Keep the leaves whole.
3. To blanch broccoli, wash florets and microwave for a minute. Sprinkle a pinch of salt and lemon juice on it immediately and mix well.
4. Chop the stems of the mushrooms in level with the caps.
5. Cut baby corns into slants, of about ½" thickness.
6. Cut the tomato into four pieces and remove pulp. Cut each piece into two.
7. Heat 1 tbsp olive oil in a non stick pan. Add the mushrooms and stir on medium heat for 2-3 minutes till well coated in oil and light brown on all sides. Add a pinch of salt. Remove to a salad bowl.
8. In the same pan heat 1 tbsp oil and saute baby corns on medium heat for 2-3 minutes. Add a pinch of salt. Remove to the salad bowl with the mushrooms. Similarly saute the zucchini also in the same way. Add zucchini and broccoli to the salad bowl.
9. Pour the prepared dressing over the warm salad in the bowl, toss to mix well. Keep aside till serving time.
10. At serving time, remove spinach from ice cold water and pat dry or roll in a clean kitchen towel. Add spinach leaves and tomatoes to the salad bowl and lightly toss.
11. Roast the sesame seeds slightly on a hot tawa. Garnish the salad with roasted seeds and serve immediately.

Warm Winter Salad

Serves 4

100 gm (30-35) small, tender spinach leaves - dipped in ice cold water for 1-2 hours
100 gm button mushrooms, choose small ones
50 gm baby corns (3-4 pieces), 4-5 florets of broccoli - blanched
6-8 thick slices of zucchini - halved, 1 firm tomato or 3-4 cherry tomatoes, halved
3 tbsp olive oil or any cooking oil

DRESSING
1 tbsp lemon juice, 2 tbsp orange juice
4 tbsp any cooking oil
1 tsp honey, 2 flakes garlic - crushed and chopped
6-8 ginger juliennes, ¼ tsp salt and ¼ tsp pepper

GARNISH, OPTIONAL
1 tbsp roasted sesame seeds (*til*) - roasted

1. Prepare the dressing by mixing, lemon juice, orange juice, oil, garlic, salt and pepper. with a whisk till it turns thick. Keep aside.
2. Remove the stems of spinach leaves. Keep the leaves whole.
3. To blanch broccoli, wash florets and microwave for a minute. Sprinkle a pinch of salt and lemon juice on it immediately and mix well.
4. Chop the stems of the mushrooms in level with the caps.
5. Cut baby corns into slants, of about ½" thickness.
6. Cut the tomato into four pieces and remove pulp. Cut each piece into two.
7. Heat 1 tbsp olive oil in a non stick pan. Add the mushrooms and stir on medium heat for 2-3 minutes till well coated in oil and light brown on all sides. Add a pinch of salt. Remove to a salad bowl.
8. In the same pan heat 1 tbsp oil and saute baby corns on medium heat for 2-3 minutes. Add a pinch of salt. Remove to the salad bowl with the mushrooms. Similarly saute the zucchini also in the same way. Add zucchini and broccoli to the salad bowl.
9. Pour the prepared dressing over the warm salad in the bowl, toss to mix well. Keep aside till serving time.
10. At serving time, remove spinach from ice cold water and pat dry or roll in a clean kitchen towel. Add spinach leaves and tomatoes to the salad bowl and lightly toss.
11. Roast the sesame seeds slightly on a hot tawa. Garnish the salad with roasted seeds and serve immediately.

Yogurt-Mayo Salad

Serves 4-6

2 boneless chicken breasts, 1 tbsp lemon juice, 1 tbsp cornflour
3 coloured capsicums, red, yellow and green
1 small cucumber - peeled & cut into cubes
1 onion - cubed and layers separated
1 lettuce head - torn into 2-3" pieces and dipped in ice cold water

VINAIGRETTE DRESSING
4 tbsp oil (vegetable oil or olive oil or salad oil)
2 tbsp vinegar or lemon juice
½ tsp salt, ½ tsp powdered sugar, ½ tsp pepper

YOGURT & MAYONNAISE DRESSING
½ cup yogurt (*dahi*), 1 cup mayonnaise
1 tsp mustard sauce, 1-2 tsp red chilli sauce

GARNISH
2 hard boiled eggs - each cut into 4 pieces

1. Cut the breast into thin juliennes. Sprinkle lemon juice and cornflour and keep aside for 10 minutes. Boil 6 cups water with 2 tsp salt and add half of the chicken strips to it. Boil for a minute or two till whitish. Check a piece for dineness and remove from water. Boil chicken and keep aside in a strainer for the excess water to drain out.
2. In a bowl put all ingredients of the vinaigrette and whisk with a baloon whisk till emulsified. Add the boiled chicken, cucumber, capsicum, onion.
3. Keep covered in the fridge for ½ hour. Toss once in between.
4. Remove the salad bowl from the fridge and drain the excess dressing from the bottom of the salad bowl.
5. Pat dry or roll lettuce in a clean kitchen towel. Add cubed tomatoes and lettuce to salad.
6. Beat yogurt till smooth and mix all ingredients of yogurt-mayonnaise dressing. Add to salad. Mix gently with a fork.
7. Garnish with chopped boiled eggs. Serve cold.

Russian Salad

Chicken and pineapple tidbits go well together. For vegetarians, omit chicken and add 1 potato, cut into small pieces and boiled in salted water.

Serves 4-6

300 gms chicken with bones or 1 large potato
1 tbsp vinegar, 1 tbsp oil
½ cup peas (*matar*)
2 carrots - diced neatly into small cubes (1½ cups)
8-10 french beans - chopped (½ cup)
½ capsicum - cut into ¼" cubes
4-5 slices of pineapple (tinned)
salt and pepper to taste

DRESSING

¾ cup mayonnaise, ¼ cup fresh cream
1 cube cheese - grated (4 tbsp) OR 1 tbsp cheese spread
½ tsp salt, ½ tsp pepper

1. To boil chicken, put it with ½ cup water and ½ tsp salt in a pressure cooker. Pressure cook to give 1 whistle and simmer on low heat for 1-2 minutes. Remove from fire. Let the pressure drop by itself. Remove meat from bones and cut into small pieces. Put in a bowl and sprinkle 1 tbsp vinegar and 1 tbsp oil on it. Keep aside for 15 minutes. If using potatoes, peel and cut potato into ½" pieces and boil in salted water. Drain, pat dry potatoes with a kitchen towel. Marinate them with oil and vinegar too.

2. Boil 2 cups water with ½ tsp salt. Add peas. As soon as the boil returns, keep boiling for 2 minutes or till peas are tender. Add the beans and carrots and boil further for 1 minute only. Remove from fire and strain. Add fresh water and strain again. Keep vegetables aside.

3. Mix mayonnaise, cream, cheese spread, salt and pepper. Mix well.

4. Squeeze pineapple slices well to remove excess syrup. Chop finely.

5. Add shredded chicken or potato, chopped pineapple, boiled vegetables and capsicum to the mayonnaise. Mix well.

6. Taste and adjust seasonings if needed. Add more pepper if required. Keep aside till serving time.

7. To serve, add a little milk to the salad if it appears extra thick. Pile the salad in the platter, forming a pyramid (heap). Serve chilled.

NOTE: The left over tinned pineapple can be stored in a plastic or steel box in the freezer of the refrigerator for 2-3 months.

From The Oven
TIPS FOR BAKING & GRILLING

Baked Dishes

Always remember to switch on the oven 15 minutes before putting the food inside, to preheat the oven. In baked dishes, most of the cooking has already been done as the sauce has been cooked, the meat & vegetables have been sauteed or boiled. The precooked things are then just assembled together in a baking dish. Thus the baking time should not be too long, but about for 15-20 minutes at 200°-250°C till the topping turns brown or the cheese melts. If the dish is kept for a longer time in a slow oven, the fat separates and the sauce loses its smooth texture. Timing and temperature, both are very important in baked casseroles. If the dish has been prepared before hand and refrigerated, the baking time will be 5 minutes more than the time stated since all the baking time given is for a dish at room temperature.

Grilled Recipes

To Grill Chicken, it is advisable to take a small broiler chicken. Keep chicken in the oven at 210°-250°C for 5-10 minutes to brown quickly on both sides. Reduce heat to 180°-200°C and grill for 15 minutes on low temperature to ensure that the chicken is cooked through. Baste with oil or butter in between.

To Grill Mutton, marinate the mutton first with a tenderizer, like raw papaya paste, for about 2 hours. Scrape off the paste after 2 hours and then marinate again with the marinade of your choice. Grill at 200°C for 1-½ hours.

To Grill Fish, heat oven to 200°C-210°C. Season fish with salt and pepper and brush with melted butter. Grill for 2 minutes on each side and then lower heat to 180°C and grill until tender.

Toppings for Baked Dishes

These toppings are done to give the delectable final touch to any baked dish.

- Sprinkle some finely chopped parsley or coriander on top.
- Dredge the dish with bread crumbs and then arrange tomato slices, overlapping one another on one side only. Sprinkle some crushed peppercorns on tomatoes.
- Top with a layer of boiled and mashed potatoes mixed with butter. Make lines or impressions with a fork. Bake till the potato topping turns crisp and golden.
- For a crisp topping, crumble fresh bread in a mixer. Remove from mixer. Add some melted butter to it and spread on the top.
- For a tempting cheesy topping, pour 1-2 tbsp of melted butter over the grated cheese before putting in the oven.

Accompaniments to Grills

Glazed Vegetables — Cut the vegetables like beans, carrots, potatoes, cauliflower and broccoli etc. into small cubes or in bigger pieces. Boil in salted water for just a few minutes till crisp-tender. Strain and refresh in cold water. Leave in the strainer till serving time. Before serving, heat some butter in a pan and add 1 tsp of sugar to the melted butter. Stir and add vegetables. Mix well to coat vegetables with butter. Sprinkle salt & white pepper.

Parsley Potatoes — Peel and boil small potatoes in salted water. Saute in a little butter with a pinch of turmeric and salt on medium flame, stirring occasionally till crisp and golden on the outside. Keep the potatoes spaced out and not overlapping each other so that they turn golden brown and crisp. Add parsley and cook further for a few minutes. Serve as an accompaniment to grilled meat or fish.

Charred Tomatoes — Cut a tomato into half. Sprinkle salt and pepper on it. Heat some butter in a pan and place the tomato with the cut side down. Press till the bottom turns brown and charred. Turn the tomato and saute the tomato in butter to coat well. Serve them as it is or cut them into wedges. If you cut tomatoes, saute the tomato wedges again in hot butter for 1-2 minutes. Serve sprinkled with salt and pepper.

Rice, Spinach & Mushroom Casserole

Serves 8-10

RICE LAYER
1 cup rice - washed and strained, keep aside in the strainer for 30 minutes
2 tbsp oil, ½ tsp cumin seeds (*jeera*), 1 onion - cut into slices
1 tsp salt, a pinch of dry mango powder (*amchoor*), ¼ tsp garam masala

MUSHROOM LAYER
200 gm mushrooms - cut into slices
1 tbsp butter, ¼ salt and ½ tsp freshly ground pepper

SPINACH LAYER
1 bundle (600 gm) spinach (*paalak*) - chopped
1 tomato - chopped, ½ tsp salt, ½ tsp pepper, ½ tsp sugar
2 tbsp butter, ¼ cup milk
2 cloves (*laung*) - crushed, seeds of 1 brown cardamom (*moti elaichi*) - crushed

TOPPING
1 cup grated cheese (mix mozarella & cheddar), 6-8 peppercorns (*saboot kali mirch*) - crushed

1. Heat 2 tbsp oil. Add cumin seeds. When they turn golden, add onion slices and stir till golden brown. Add *amchoor* and garam masala. Stir till onions turn rich brown. Add rice to the onions. Stir gently for a few seconds. Add 2 cups water and salt. Boil. Cook covered on low heat for 12-13 minutes, or till the rice is done and the water gets absorbed. Remove from fire and keep aside.

2. Boil spinach and a tomato with ¼ cup water in a pan for 3-4 minutes. Remove from fire. Cool and grind to a puree. Add salt, pepper, sugar, 2 tbsp butter, milk, crushed cardamom and cloves to the spinach puree and cook for 4-5 minutes on low heat till slightly thick. Remove from fire.

3. Saute mushrooms in 1 tbsp butter for 4-5 minutes till water evaporates and they turn brown. Add salt & pepper to taste.

4. To assemble, grease an oven proof dish. Spread the rice first, covering about ½ the height of the dish. Do not fill the dish too much with rice. Raise the sides a little by spreading some rice from the centre to the sides.

5. Then put all the spinach in the centre and spread, a little away from the edges, such that the rice shows on the sides. Finally top spinach with sauteed mushrooms.

6. Sprinkle cheese. Garnish with tomato slices. Sprinkle crushed peppercorns. To serve, bake the dish in a preheated oven at 180°C for about 10 minutes till cheese melts. Serve hot.

Moussaka

A classic Greek dish of aubergines and minced lamb.

Serves 6-8

2-3 aubergines (brinjals), thin long variety
2 tomatoes - blanched and chopped, 500 gm lamb mince (keema)
2 large onions - finely chopped, 4-6 flakes garlic - crushed & chopped finely
2 tbsp tomato puree, 4-5 tbsp olive oil or any cooking oil
½ tsp red chilli flakes, ½ tsp oregano, ¼ tsp pepper, 1 tsp salt or to taste

CHEESE SAUCE
2 tbsp butter, 3 tbsp plain flour (*maida*), 1¼ cups (275-300 ml) milk, 1 egg
1 cube cheese - grated (4 tbsp), salt to taste, ½ tsp mustard paste

1. Thinly slice the aubergines (*baingan*) and arrange them in a large plate. Sprinkle salt on both sides. Let the aubergines stand for ½ hour to drain out juices. Rinse the aubergine slices in cold water and pat dry.
2. Heat 1 cup oil in a kadhai or frying pan and fry the aubergine slices until brown. Drain on paper napkins or absorbent paper. Keep aside.
3. Put tomatoes in boiling water for 2 minutes. Drain. Peel the outer skin. Chop finely.
4. Heat 4-5 tbsp oil in a pressure cooker, add the chopped onion and stir.
5. Add the garlic and cook till the onions turn pink. Add the tomatoes, stir fry till the juices evaporate and tomatoes turn dry. Add the mince and cook on high flame until brown and dry. Add tomato puree, chilli flakes, oregano, salt & pepper. Add ½ to ¾ cup of water and pressure cook to give one whistle, reduce the flame and simmer for 1-2 minutes. Remove from flame. Cool.
6. Check for tenderness and cook till almost dry. Dry the excess liquid but do not make it too dry. Adjust the seasoning according to taste. Keep aside.
7. To prepare the cheese sauce, heat butter in a heavy bottomed pan, add flour, stir gently on low flame for 1 minute till it slightly changes colour. Remove from heat. Add the milk and mix well. Return to heat and cook till the sauce becomes thick. Add salt, pepper, mustard and cheese. Remove from heat and cool slightly.
8. Add the beaten egg to the cooled white sauce. Keep aside.
9. To assemble, spoon half of the meat mixture in a shallow ovenproof dish. Top with half the aubergine slices. Repeat with the remaining meat and aubergines slices. Then pour the cheese sauce. Cook in a preheated oven at 200°C for 25-30 minutes or until bubbling hot and browned. Serve with garlic bread.

Baked Fish in Cheese Custard

Serves 8

½ kg fish, preferably boneless - boiled and flaked
1 bay leaf (*tej patta*)
1 onion - chopped
2 to 3 flakes garlic - crushed and chopped
2 cloves (*laung*) - crushed
salt & pepper to taste
2 tomatoes - sliced
2 eggs - beaten well with a little salt & pepper
2 cubes cheese (50 gm) - grated
½ cup milk - hot
1 tbsp butter

SAUCE

3 tbsp butter
3 tbsp plain flour (*maida*)
2 cups milk
½ tsp salt, ¼ tsp pepper, or to taste

1. Boil fish by placing it in a covered vessel with 1 cup water, ½ tsp salt and 1 bay leaf for 10 minutes on low flame after the first boil. Strain and keep stock aside. Debone and flake the fish.
2. Prepare the sauce by melting butter in a heavy bottomed pan. Add flour and stir for a minute. Add the milk, stirring continuously. Add the left over stock. Cook, stirring continuously till slightly thick.
3. Add ½ tsp salt and ¼ tsp pepper, or to taste. Remove from fire. Keep aside.
4. Heat 1 tbsp butter, add onion. Cook till transparent. Add garlic and crushed cloves.
5. Add fish flakes. Add salt and pepper to taste. Cook for 2 minutes. Remove from fire and spread in an oven proof serving dish.
6. Pour hot white sauce over the fish covering it well.
7. Arrange tomato slices on the white sauce and sprinkle some pepper.
8. Pour beaten eggs over the tomato slices.
9. Beat grated cheese with hot milk and pour over the eggs.
10. Dot with butter and bake in a preheated medium hot oven, at about 200°C for about 30 minutes till the top turns golden brown.

Cauliflower & Broccoli Bake

Serves 4-6

250 gm (½ of a medium) cauliflower
150 gm (1 small flower) broccoli
juice of 1 lemon
2 tbsp butter
½ cup tinned corn kernels
½ tsp peppercorns (*saboot kali mirch*) - crushed

CORIANDER-CHEESE SAUCE
2 tbsp butter
¼ tsp carom seeds (*ajwain*)
3-4 flakes garlic - crushed
1 small onion - chopped finely
2 tbsp plain flour (*maida*)
2¼ cups milk
2 tbsp chopped coriander, 4 tbsp grated cheese
¾ tsp salt and ¼ tsp pepper, or to taste

1. Cut cauliflower and broccoli into medium florets with small stalks.
2. Boil 5-6 cups water with a 2 tsp salt, 1 tsp sugar and juice of 1 lemon. Add florets to boiling water. As soon as the boil returns, remove from fire. Leave vegetables in hot water for 2 minutes. Drain. Do not over cook. Refresh in cold water. Pat dry on a clean kitchen towel or a paper napkin.
3. Heat butter and saute the florets till dry, for about 3-4 minutes. Keep them spaced out while sauteing and do not overlap the pieces. Saute, stirring very little, till brown specs appear on the cauliflower. Remove from butter and arrange in an ovenproof serving dish.
4. Squeeze the tinned corn and arrange corn over the florets in the dish. Sprinkle corn with half the crushed peppercorns.
5. To prepare white sauce, melt butter in a heavy bottomed pan. Add carom seeds. Wait for a minute and add garlic. Stir and add onion. Cook till onion turns soft. Add flour. Cook on slow fire for 1-2 minutes. Remove from fire.
6. Add milk gradually, stirring continuously. Return to fire. Stir till it boils. Cook for 2-3 minutes on low heat. Do not make it too thick. Add coriander and 2 tbsp cheese. Add salt and pepper to taste. Remove from fire.
7. Spread the white sauce over the cauliflower, broccoli and corn. Sprinkle some grated cheese and crushed peppercorns.
8. Bake at 220°C/475°F for 20 minutes till light brown. Serve immediately.

Serves 5-6

100 gm baby corns, fresh or tinned - sliced into 2 lengthways
125 gm (12-15) small sized mushrooms (fresh or tinned) - cut the stem into round slices and the top into 2 pieces horizontally
1 carrot - peeled and cut into small cubes
1 onion - finely sliced, 2 tbsp butter
3-4 tbsp grated cheese, optional

HERBED WHITE SAUCE
2 tbsp butter
2 tbsp plain flour (*maida*), 2½ cups milk
¾ tsp salt, ¼ tsp pepper, ¼ tsp paprika
2 tbsp finely chopped mint or parsley or dill (soye)
½ cup boiled peas
¼ tsp grated nutmeg

1. For fresh baby corns and carrots, boil 3 cups water with 1 tsp salt. Add baby corns and carrots. Boil for about 2 minutes, after the first boil. Remove vegetables with a slotted spoon. If you are using tinned baby corns, there is no need to boil them.
2. For fresh mushrooms, add 2 tsp lemon juice to the above water and boil again. Add mushrooms and boil for 2-3 minutes on medium flame. Drain. There is no need to boil tinned mushrooms.
3. Melt 2 tbsp butter in a nonstick pan and add onions and fry till brown. Remove from butter and keep aside.
4. Saute mushrooms in the same pan in the remaining butter for 3 minutes till light brown. Remove from pan and keep aside.
5. In the same pan, saute the baby corns and carrots for 2 minutes till brown specs appear on the corns. Remove from pan and keep aside.
6. To prepare herbed white sauce, melt 2 tbsp butter in the same pan. Add flour and cook on low flame for 1-2 minutes. Remove from fire.
7. Gradually add milk, stirring continuously.
8. Return to fire. Boil. Add peas. Simmer for 2 minutes. Add salt, pepper and nutmeg. Remove from fire. Add mint or parsley or dill.
9. To assemble, grease an oven proof dish. Spread 3-4 tbsp white sauce first at the bottom of the dish. Spread a few fried onions.
10. Keeping aside 3-4 baby corn pieces for garnishing, spread the rest of baby corns, and all the carrots and mushrooms over it. Cover with herbed sauce.
11. Sprinkle some onions. Sprinkle cheese. Arrange the whole baby corns in one corner. Bake at 220°C for 15 minutes or till light brown. Serve hot.

Grilled Fish with Tangy Sauce

Fish marinated with olive oil, lemon juice, garlic and herbs and later grilled and served with a sauce.

Serves 2-3

300-350 gm fish fillets (sole, boneless)
2 cubes cheese - grated, optional

MARINADE

2-3 tbsp olive oil, 2 tbsp lemon juice, 3-4 garlic flakes - crushed
½ tsp freshly crushed peppercorns, ½ tsp salt or to taste
a pinch of orange colour
½ tsp mixed herbs (basil & thyme) or dried oregano or 1 tsp fresh basil

TANGY SAUCE

2-3 green olives - finely chopped
1-2 tsp lemon juice
2 tbsp olive oil or any cooking oil
½ tsp finely chopped ginger
2 tbsp cornflour mixed with 1 cup water
½ tsp salt or to taste, ½ tsp freshly crushed peppercorns
1 tsp sugar, ¼ tsp chilli flakes
4 tbsp cream

GARNISH

lemon wedges
fresh dill (soye) or basil leaves

1. Mix all the ingredients of the marinade.
2. Wash the fish fillets and pat dry. Marinate the fillets with marinade and keep aside in the refrigerator to marinate for 1 hour, turning sides once or twice in between.
3. Grill the fish fillet in a baking dish at 200°C for 15-20 minutes, turning side gently once in between. Just before removing from the oven, sprinkle cheese and grill again for 2-3 minutes.
4. Meanwhile make the sauce. Heat oil in a pan and add the ginger. Stir for ½ minute on low heat. Add cornflour paste and stir continuously till it coats the back of the spoon. Add salt, pepper, sugar and red chilli flakes. Cook till well blended and remove from heat. Add olives and cream. Finish with lemon juice.
5. Serve the baked fish fillets with the sauce.
6. Garnish with lemon wedges, fresh dill or basil sprigs. Serve hot with french fries and a salad if you like.

French Egg Casserole

Eggs served on a bed of crisp onions and topped with white sauce & cheese.

Serves 4

2 hard boiled eggs - cut lengthwise into halves
2 large onions - sliced and deep fried to a golden brown colour
½ cup shelled & boiled peas
2 tbsp dry bread crumbs

WHITE SAUCE (THIN SAUCE)
3 tbsp butter, 2 tbsp plain flour (*maida*)
3½ cups milk
1 cube (25 gm) cheese - grated
salt, pepper to taste

1. Prepare the white sauce by melting butter in a heavy bottomed pan. Add flour and stir for a minute. Remove from fire.
2. Add the milk, stirring continuously. Return to fire. Cook, stirring continuously till slightly thick. Add cheese, salt and pepper to taste. Remove from fire and keep the white sauce aside.
3. To assemble the casserole, arrange a layer of fried onions to cover the bottom of the baking dish. Arrange eggs on it.
4. Mix boiled peas with the prepared white sauce.
5. Pour the white sauce over the eggs.
6. Dredge with bread crumbs.
7. Bake for about 10 minutes, on the top rack of a hot oven till the dish gets browned Serve hot with buttered toasts.

Lemon Fish Florentine

Serves 4

8 pieces (300-400 gm) - Sole (boneless) fillets
300-400 gm spinach
1½ tbsp butter, 1 tbsp lemon juice, salt & freshly crushed black peppercorns to taste

SAUCE

3 tbsp butter, 3 tbsp plain flour (*maida*), 2¼ cups (450 ml) milk
¼ tsp salt, ½ tsp peppercorns - coarsely crushed
½ cup grated cheese (parmesan or cheddar)

1. Remove the stem of the spinach leaves and shred the leaves thickly. Wash well and strain. Squeeze the excess water. Keep aside.
2. Wash and pat dry the fish fillet on a paper towel and marinate with lemon juice, salt and pepper. Keep aside for ½ hour.
3. Heat 1 tbsp butter in a non stick pan and add the fish fillet. Lightly fry the pieces on both sides on medium heat, till light brown and cooked. Drain, keep aside.
4. In the sauce pan, add ½ tbsp of butter and cook the shredded spinach till all the water evaporates. Keep spinach aside.
5. To prepare the sauce, heat a clean pan. Add 3 tbsp butter. When it melts add the flour & cook on low flame till it slightly changes colour. Remove from heat & add the milk. Mix well & return to heat. Cook till the sauce thickens. Add salt & pepper to taste.
6. Stir half of the sauce into the cooked spinach mixture.
7. Arrange the cooked fish pieces in a shallow ovenproof dish. Spread the spinach over the fish. Pour the remaining sauce over the fish and top with grated cheese. Bake in a preheated oven at 200°C for 15-20 minutes or till cheese melts. Serve hot with lemon or garlic bread.

Quiche Lorraine

Serves 6

SHORTCRUST PASTRY (BASE)
150 gm plain flour (*maida*), 75-80 gm chilled butter
¼ tsp salt, 2 tbsp cold water, 8" flan dish or loose bottom tin

FILLING
2 tbsp butter, 1 large onion - chopped, 150 gm mushrooms - chopped
200 gm spinach - shredded, 5-6 cubes (100-125 gm) cheddar cheese - grated
2-3 green chillies - chopped, salt and pepper to taste
200 gm cream (pouring consistency), 1 egg, 2 tsp cornflour

1. To prepare the base, sift the flour and salt in a bowl. Take cold butter and cut into small pieces. Add butter to the flour and rub it lightly with the finger tips with the flour until the mixture looks like fine bread crumbs. Add 1-2 tbsp of cold water and form a firm soft dough (not sticky). Keep wrapped in cling film or covered in a damp cloth for 15-20 minutes in a refrigerator.

2. Roll out the flour into a round of 10" diameter & 1/8" thickness. Place the rolled out dough in the flan dish or tin. Press on the sides and bottom. Prick the bottom with a fork. You can also use small, individual serving quiche tins as shown in the picture.

3. Line the pastry with aluminium foil by placing the foil over the pastry base and covering the sides too. Throw 1 cup of dry kidney beans (rajma) over the foil. The weight of the beans ensures that the pastry does not puff up during baking. Remember to put the beans on the edges too.

4. Place the flan in preheated oven at 210°C-220°C and bake blind (without filling) for 15-20 minutes. Remove from oven and remove the foil with beans and bake the shell again for 10 minutes until the pastry is dry and light brown. Remove from oven and keep the base or shell aside to cool.

5. To prepare the filling, melt 1 tbsp butter in a pan. Add the onions and cook gently till light brown. Add chopped mushrooms and cook for 2-3 minutes. Add green chillies, salt and pepper and cook till all the water from the mushrooms evaporates.

6. Spoon the mushroom mixture in the prepared pastry shell and spread evenly.

7. Heat 1 tbsp butter in the sauce pan, add shredded spinach and cook till all the water evaporates. Add a pinch of salt. Spoon over the onion and mushroom mixture.

8. Spread grated cheese over the mushroom-spinach mixture.

9. Beat egg. Add cream and cornflour to the beaten egg. Pour it over the cheese in pastry shell.

10. Reduce the oven temperature to 180°C and bake the shell with the filling for 25-30 minutes until filling is golden brown and set. Serve hot.

Serves 4

1 small chicken (650-700 gm) - cut into 4 or 8 pieces

1ST MARINADE

2 tbsp vinegar, 1 tbsp oil, ½ tsp salt

2ND MARINADE

2-3 tbsp butter - softened
1 small onion - very finely chopped (4 tbsp)
2-3 mushrooms - very finely chopped, minced (4-5 tbsp)
1 tsp mixed dried herbs (oregano, basil, thyme, sage, tarragon)
¼ tsp salt, ½ tsp freshly ground pepper
2-3 tbsp fine dried bread crumbs

1. Wash and pat dry the chicken pieces. Marinate the chicken with the first marinade - vinegar, oil and salt for 1-2 hours in the refrigerator.

2. To prepare the second marinade, slightly melt the butter if too solid. Add very finely chopped mushrooms and onion, any herb, salt and freshly ground pepper. Mix well and spread evenly on the chicken pieces. Keep aside for 1 hour or till the time of cooking.

3. Heat oven to 210°C. Place chicken on a baking tray and place the tray in the oven for 5-7 minutes, keeping it a little distant from heat.

4. Remove the tray from the oven. Baste with a little melted butter if the chicken seems dry. Sprinkle bread crumbs over the pieces and reduce heat to 150°C. Place the tray back in oven and grill for 15-20 minutes till chicken turns tender. If you like the chicken very soft, cover the chicken with aluminium foil and then grill. Serve hot with a salad (page 20) and parsley potatoes, as on page 25.

Bean & Spinach Bake

Serves 8

200 gm mushrooms - trim stalks and cut each into 4-5 'T' shaped slices
100 gm baby corns - cut into ¼" thick round slices
3 tbsp butter, 4-5 cups (½ bundle) finely chopped spinach leaves
1 cup tinned baked beans in sauce
½ tsp red chilli flakes, salt & pepper to taste
4 tbsp dried bread crumbs, 50 gm mozzarella cheese - grated

SAUCE

1½ tbsp cornflour mixed with 1½ cups milk, 1 tbsp butter
½ onion - finely chopped, 3-4 flakes garlic - crushed, 2 green chillies - chopped
¾ tsp salt and 6-8 peppercorns - crushed, or to taste

1. Wash and strain the spinach to drain out all water. Leave the spinach in the strainer for 15 minutes. In a pan, add 1 tbsp of butter and cook the shredded spinach and cook till all the water evaporates. Stir fry for 2-3 minutes till it gets fried. Add bread crumbs and mix well. (Bread crumbs prevent the spinach from turning runny). Add salt and pepper to taste. Transfer to a shallow serving dish.

2. Spread a layer of baked beans on it.

3. Heat 2 tbsp butter. Add mushrooms and baby corns and saute for 5-7 minutes till brown specs appear. Add red chilli flakes and salt-pepper to taste.

4. Arrange the baby corns and mushrooms on the baked beans.

5. For the sauce, heat butter and add onion and stir for a minute. Add garlic and green chillies and again give a quick stir. Add cornflour mixed with milk and stir continuously till sauce turns thick and starts coating the back of the spoon. Remove sauce from fire and pour over the baby corns and mushrooms. Grate cheese on top. Bake for 15 minutes at 200°C.

A Swiss style of making a potato and mushroom pancake, topped with cheese and grilled.

Makes 4

4 large potatoes - boiled in salted water for about 10 minutes, till just cooked and peeled & cooled in the refrigerator
½ tbsp butter, ½ onion - chopped very finely, 6-7 mushrooms - chopped finely
1 tbsp finely chopped parsley, 2 tbsp cornflour, ¾ tsp salt and ¼ tsp pepper
2 tbsp olive oil or any other cooking oil and 2 tbsp butter
8 tbsp grated cheese

1. Melt ½ tbsp butter in a pan. Add onions and mushrooms and cook for 3-4 minutes till they turn light brown and dry. Add ¼ tsp salt and a little pepper.
2. Grate cold potatoes coarsely. Add mushrooms, parsley, cornflour, salt and pepper. Lightly mix everything well with a fork. Check seasonings. Keep aside.
3. Melt ½ tbsp oil and ½ tbsp butter in a large, heavy pan over medium heat. Add ¼ of the potato mixture and spread out into a thick pancake, taking care not to press it down too much. Neaten the edges by pushing the potatoes from the sides towards the centre. Cook on medium heat till the edges of the pancake starts to brown. Loosen the edges. Shake the pan once gently. Reduce heat and further cook on low heat for 2-3 minutes till the underside turns brown and crisp. Now slide the pancake carefully into a plate. Put some oil and butter again in the pan. Carefully hold the plate above the empty pan and quickly invert the plate so that the pancake falls on the pan with the cooked side up. Cook the other side also till both sides are light golden. Remove from fire and gently slide from the pan to an oven proof platter.
4. Sprinkle 2 tbsp grated cheese on each rosti. Keep in the oven at about 200°C for 5-7 minutes or till cheese turns golden. Serve hot with mushroom pate if you like

Mushroom Pate

Serves 6

200 gm mushrooms - chopped roughly
2 tbsp butter, 1 small onion - finely chopped
½ tsp coriander (*dhania*) powder, 1 tbsp brandy, optional
4 tbsp cheese spread
¼ cup hung curd (hang ½ cup thick curd in a muslin for 30 minutes)
½ tsp salt and ½ tsp freshly ground pepper, or to taste

1. Melt butter. Add ground coriander and onion. Stir until onions turn soft.
2. Add chopped mushrooms and stir for about 3 minutes until the mushrooms are slightly cooked. Add brandy and cook further for 2 minutes. Remove from fire.
3. Put the mushrooms in a blender. Add the cheese spread, hung curd, salt and pepper to taste. Blend to a smooth puree. Transfer to a bowl. Check salt and pepper.

Pancake Florentine

Serves 6

PANCAKES
¾ plain flour (*maida*), 1 egg, 1½ cups milk, approx., ¼ tsp salt

FILLING
100 gm mushrooms - sliced thinly
350 gm (½ bundle) spinach - discard stems and chop finely (4 cups)
1½ tbsp butter
3 cubes (60 gm) cheddar cheese - grated
salt & pepper to taste, 1 tsp lemon juice

RED SAUCE
1 tbsp butter
3 tomatoes - blanched and chopped
3-4 flakes garlic - crushed and chopped
1 tbsp tomato ketchup, ½ tsp red chilli flakes
a pinch of sugar, ½ tsp salt

WHITE SAUCE
1½ tbsp butter
1¼ tbsp flour (*maida*), 1½ cups of milk (300 ml)
¼ tsp each of salt & pepper, or to taste

1. To prepare the pancake batter, sift flour and salt in a bowl. Make a well in the centre and add the egg and ½ cup milk. Beat or mix well to make a smooth thick batter. Beat again for 1-2 minutes so that not lumps are formed. Cover and leave to stand for ½ hour. After keeping aside for 30 minutes, add rest of the milk, adding enough to get a thin coating consistency batter. Mix well.

2. To cook the pancakes, melt a little, about ½ tsp of butter in a non stick pan.

3. Remove pan from fire and pour a small kadchi (about 3 tbsp) of batter. Tilt and rotate the pan gently to get a thin even layer of the batter covering the base of the pan. The pancakes should be thin so put only a small amount of the batter in the pan, just enough batter to coat the pan.

4. Cook on medium flame till set. When the pancake looks cooked, loosen from the sides of the pan and check lifting the pancake that it is slight brown from underneath. Remove the pancake from the pan to a plate. Repeat with the other pancakes, cooking them on one side only. Keep them covered.

5. To prepare the red sauce, place the tomatoes in a pan with 1½ cups of water and boil for 3-4 minutes. Drain and cool under cold water. Remove the outer skin and chop finely.

6. Heat butter in a pan and add the garlic. Stir and add the tomatoes. Mix well. Add chilli flakes, salt, sugar and ¼ cup of water. Simmer for a minute and add the tomato sauce. Check the seasoning and cook till slightly thick. Remove from fire.
7. To prepare the white sauce, heat butter in a pan. Add flour and stir for 1 minute on low heat till it changes colour. Remove from heat and add the milk. Return to heat and cook till it starts to coat the spoon. Do not make it too thick. Add salt and pepper. Keep aside.
8. Heat 1 tsp butter in a pan. Add the mushrooms and stir for 2-3 minutes. Sprinkle ¼ tsp each of salt and pepper. Keep aside.
9. In the same pan add 1 tbsp butter and add the spinach. Cook till all the water it leaves evaporates and it turns dry. Add salt, pepper and lemon juice. Remove from heat when dry.
10. Mix the mushrooms and spinach together and keep aside.
11. To assemble the pancakes, keep a pancake with the uncooked side down. Place some spinach-mushroom mixture on half the side. Turn the other side and then fold again to get triangles. Repeat with the remaining pancakes.
12. Grease a shallow oblong or a rectangular baking dish with a little butter. Spread 2-3 tbsp white sauce at the base of the dish.
13. Place the stuffed pancakes side by side, top with the red sauce and then with white sauce.
14. Sprinkle the remaining grated cheese. Place in a moderately hot oven at 200°C for 10-12 minutes. Serve with garlic bread or buns.

Chicken Amandine

A creamy chicken with macaroni, topped with toasted almonds.

Serves 4-5

250-300 gm boneless chicken - cut into 1" pieces
50 gm macaroni (½ cup)
1 tbsp butter
1 small capsicum - deseeded and chopped
1 small firm tomato - deseeded and chopped

SAUCE

1 small onion - chopped
2 tbsp butter, 2½ tbsp flour (*maida*)
1½ cups chicken stock
4 tbsp tomato puree, 1 tbsp tomato ketchup
4 tbsp fresh cream
salt and pepper to taste
2 tbsp chopped parsley or coriander

GARNISH

3-4 almonds - cut into thin long pieces
some grated cheese

1. Heat 1 tbsp butter in a pressure cooker. Add the chicken pieces and stir fry for 2-3 minutes. Add 1½ cups water and pressure cook to give 2 whistles. Reduce heat and simmer for 1-2 minutes. Remove from heat. Cool. Strain and reserve the stock for sauce and keep the chicken pieces aside.

2. Boil 2 cups of water. Add macaroni and boil for 7-8 minutes till tender. Drain and refresh under cold water. Strain and keep aside in the strainer for all the water to drain out.

3. To prepare the sauce, heat butter in a pan and add onions. Stir till they turn soft and slightly change colour. Add the flour and stir till light brown. Mix stock and milk to get 3 cups (550-600 ml). Lower heat and add the stock-milk mixture. Stir till smooth and creamy. Remove from heat. Add tomato puree, tomato ketchup, cream, salt, pepper and chopped parsley or coriander.

4. Add macaroni, chicken, capsicum and tomato. Stir well and check the seasoning, adjust according to taste.

5. Pour the mixture in a baking dish. Top with grated cheese and almonds. Heat in a moderate oven at 180°C for 5-7 minutes. Serve hot with buttered toasts and cut into triangles.

6. Heat butter in a pan and add the garlic. Stir and add the tomatoes. Mix well. Add chilli flakes, salt, sugar and ¼ cup of water. Simmer for a minute and add the tomato sauce. Check the seasoning and cook till slightly thick. Remove from fire.

7. To prepare the white sauce, heat butter in a pan. Add flour and stir for 1 minute on low heat till it changes colour. Remove from heat and add the milk. Return to heat and cook till it starts to coat the spoon. Do not make it too thick. Add salt and pepper. Keep aside.

8. Heat 1 tsp butter in a pan. Add the mushrooms and stir for 2-3 minutes. Sprinkle ¼ tsp each of salt and pepper. Keep aside.

9. In the same pan add 1 tbsp butter and add the spinach. Cook till all the water it leaves evaporates and it turns dry. Add salt, pepper and lemon juice. Remove from heat when dry.

10. Mix the mushrooms and spinach together and keep aside.

11. To assemble the pancakes, keep a pancake with the uncooked side down. Place some spinach-mushroom mixture on half the side. Turn the other side and then fold again to get triangles. Repeat with the remaining pancakes.

12. Grease a shallow oblong or a rectangular baking dish with a little butter. Spread 2-3 tbsp white sauce at the base of the dish.

13. Place the stuffed pancakes side by side, top with the red sauce and then with white sauce.

14. Sprinkle the remaining grated cheese. Place in a moderately hot oven at 200°C for 10-12 minutes. Serve with garlic bread or buns.

Chicken Amandine

A creamy chicken with macaroni, topped with toasted almonds.

Serves 4-5

250-300 gm boneless chicken - cut into 1" pieces
50 gm macaroni (½ cup)
1 tbsp butter
1 small capsicum - deseeded and chopped
1 small firm tomato - deseeded and chopped

SAUCE

1 small onion - chopped
2 tbsp butter, 2½ tbsp flour (*maida*)
1½ cups chicken stock
4 tbsp tomato puree, 1 tbsp tomato ketchup
4 tbsp fresh cream
salt and pepper to taste
2 tbsp chopped parsley or coriander

GARNISH

3-4 almonds - cut into thin long pieces
some grated cheese

1. Heat 1 tbsp butter in a pressure cooker. Add the chicken pieces and stir fry for 2-3 minutes. Add 1½ cups water and pressure cook to give 2 whistles. Reduce heat and simmer for 1-2 minutes. Remove from heat. Cool. Strain and reserve the stock for sauce and keep the chicken pieces aside.

2. Boil 2 cups of water. Add macaroni and boil for 7-8 minutes till tender. Drain and refresh under cold water. Strain and keep aside in the strainer for all the water to drain out.

3. To prepare the sauce, heat butter in a pan and add onions. Stir till they turn soft and slightly change colour. Add the flour and stir till light brown. Mix stock and milk to get 3 cups (550-600 ml). Lower heat and add the stock-milk mixture. Stir till smooth and creamy. Remove from heat. Add tomato puree, tomato ketchup, cream, salt, pepper and chopped parsley or coriander.

4. Add macaroni, chicken, capsicum and tomato. Stir well and check the seasoning, adjust according to taste.

5. Pour the mixture in a baking dish. Top with grated cheese and almonds. Heat in a moderate oven at 180°C for 5-7 minutes. Serve hot with buttered toasts and cut into triangles.

Chicken Casserole

Chicken baked with mushrooms, topped with white sauce, crisp bread crumbs & cheese.

Serves 4-6

1 cup boiled and shredded chicken, 100 gm mushrooms - chopped
1 cup small florets of broccoli - put in hot boiling water for a minute and refreshed in cold water, 2 onions - chopped
2 slices of bread - churned in a mixer to get crumbs
2 tbsp olive oil

WHITE SAUCE (THIN SAUCE)

3 tbsp butter, 3 tbsp plain flour (*maida*), 3 cubes (60 gm) cheese - grated
salt, pepper to taste, ½ tsp red chilli powder (optional)
3 cups milk

1. Melt butter in a heavy bottomed pan. Add onions and cook till transparent.
2. Add mushrooms. Stir for 2 minutes.
3. Sprinkle flour. Stir continuously for a minute on low heat. Remove from fire.
4. Add the milk, stirring continuously. Return to fire. Cook, stirring continuously till it coats the back of the spoon.
5. Add salt and pepper to taste. Add broccoli and bring it to a boil.
6. Add chicken and simmer for a minute.
7. Add grated cheese. Remove from heat. Transfer to a baking dish.
8. Just before baking, mix fresh bread crumbs with olive oil and sprinkle on the dish. Bake for about 20-30 minutes in a hot oven till the dish gets browned.

Baked Corn with Asparagus

Serves 8

1 cup tinned, cooked or frozen corn kernels
10-12 stalks of fresh or tinned asparagus
2 carrots - cut into small cubes
100 gm mozzarella cheese - grated

WHITE SAUCE

2½ tbsp flour
2½ tbsp butter
2½ cups milk
1 tsp salt and ¾ tsp pepper, or to taste
1 tsp oregano

1. If using fresh asparagus, snip 1½" from the lower end. If the asparagus is tough, you may also need to peel the lower stem with a peeler thinly. If tender, just snip the ends. Cut the asparagus into 2" pieces. To boil asparagus, boil 2 cups water with 1 tsp salt and ½ tsp sugar in a pan. Add asparagus and carrots. Cook uncovered on low heat for 2 minutes till tender by feeling the stem of the asparagus. Remove from water and drain. If using tinned asparagus, there is no need to boil it. Keep vegetables aside.

2. For the sauce, melt butter and stir in the flour. Stir for a minute. Gradually add the milk and bring to a boil stirring continuously. Keep on low heat for 3-4 minutes.

3. Keeping aside 4-5 upper portions of the asparagus for garnishing, add the rest of the asparagus to the white sauce. Add corn and carrots also to the sauce. Cook on low heat for 3-4 minutes till thick. Add salt and pepper to taste. Remove from fire. Add half of the grated cheese and oregano. Mix well.

4. Grease a baking dish and put the corn-carrot-asparagus mixture in it. Cover with the remaining cheese. Garnish with the remaining asparagus pieces. Bake in a hot oven at 200°C for 20 minutes or until golden. Serve hot.

Hot Cheese Souffle

Serves 4

2 tbsp butter
2 tbsp flour (*maida*)
150 ml (slightly less than 1 cup) milk
3 eggs
75 gm cheese - grated
salt, pepper and mustard powder to taste

1. Melt the butter and stir in the flour. Stir for 1 minute.
2. Gradually add the milk stirring continuously until smooth. Cook till thick.
3. Remove sauce from fire. Cool the sauce slightly.
4. Separate eggs. Add egg yolks to the cooled sauce one by one, beating well. Add cheese, salt, pepper and mustard powder.
5. Beat egg whites stiffly and fold gently into the sauce.
6. Transfer to a greased ovenproof dish or individual souffle ramekins. Bake in a moderately hot oven at 400°F/200°C, for about 20 minutes, till well risen and brown. Serve at once.

Baked Tomato Fish

Serves 4-6

½ kg white fish fillet (boneless) - cut into 2" pieces
2 tsp gram flour (*besan*) and juice of ½ lemon
½ tsp paprika or degi mirch, salt to taste, 2 tbsp cornflour

SAUCE

1 tbsp butter, 1 onion - chopped roughly
6 large tomatoes - chopped roughly
8-10 flakes garlic, 1 bay leaf (*tej patta*)
½ tsp aniseeds (*saunf*), salt to taste
2 tsp tomato ketchup, 2 tsp Worcestershire sauce
½ tsp pepper powder, ½ tsp sugar, 1 cube cheese - grated

1. Rub the fish fillet gently with 2 tsp gramflour and some lemon juice to remove the fishy odour. Wash well. Pat dry on a kitchen towel.
2. Sprinkle salt and paprika on the fish and roll it in cornflour.
3. Heat a little oil in a pan and shallow fry the fish on medium heat.
4. Remove the fish fillet from pan on to a shallow baking dish.
5. To prepare the sauce, in a pressure cooker, put onion, tomatoes, garlic, bay leaf, aniseeds, salt and ½ cup water. Pressure cook to give 1 whistle. Remove from fire.
6. Cool. Remove bay leaf. Blend the mixture to a puree in a mixer. Strain the puree.
7. Heat butter. Add the tomato puree and cook till it thickens to a saucy consistency. Add the two sauces, pepper and sugar. Remove from fire.
8. Spread the sauce on the fish pieces covering it completely. Grate cheese on top. Bake in a hot oven till cheese melts, at 200°C for 10 minutes. Serve with rice or bread.

Vegetable & Cheese Souffle

A hot souffle tastes good only if served fresh from the oven. You may work upto mixing the sauce with egg yolks and other vegetables etc. (step 3), and add beaten eggwhites about 40 minutes before serving, so as to serve it straight from the oven.

Serves 4

100 gm mixed vegetables - diced (1 cup) (carrots, peas, beans, cauliflower, broccoli)
3 tbsp butter, 1 tbsp plain flour (*maida*)
1 cup (200 ml) milk
3 eggs
3 cubes (60 gm) cheddar cheese - grated
1 green chilli - chopped finely
2 tbsp chopped parsley or coriander
¼ tsp freshly ground peppercorns
¼ tsp salt

1. Boil 2-3 cups water with 1 tsp salt. Add the diced vegetables to the boiling water. Boil for 1-2 minutes and drain immediately. Refresh the vegetables with cold water and strain. Press gently to remove excess water. Pat dry the vegetables on a kitchen towel or a paper napkin. Keep vegetables aside.
2. Melt butter in a pan on medium heat. Add flour and stir for 1 minute. Gradually add the milk and cook stirring continuously till the sauce thickens. Remove from heat and add the grated cheese. Stir and keep aside to cool.
3. When the sauce cools, separate the egg yolks and whites. Add the egg yolks one at a time to the cool sauce, mixing well after each addition. Stir in parsley, green chilli, salt & pepper and the vegetables. Mix well.
4. Whip the egg whites until stiff. Fold them carefully into the sauce.
5. Butter a souffle or a baking dish. Gently pour the prepared mixture in the dish.
6. Bake in a preheated oven at 180°C for 30-35 minutes or until well cooked. To check if the souffle is cooked, pierce with a knife. It should be well set and not soft at the bottom. If it appears soft at the bottom, make 2-3 cuts on the top to cook thoroughly till the bottom gets done. Serve hot with garlic bread.

Corn & Spinach Souffle

1. Shred 200 gm of spinach leaves. Wash and pat dry on a kitchen towel to remove excess moisture.
2. Cook in ½ tsp of butter in a pan till moisture evaporates.
3. Add ½ cup cooked spinach and ½ cup cooked corn to the prepared sauce instead of the vegetables.

Shepherd's Pie

Minced lamb baked with carrots and mushrooms or peas. Topped with mashed potatoes.

Serves 6

500 gm minced lamb (*keema*)
4-5 tbsp oil
4-6 flakes garlic - chopped finely, 2 onions - chopped finely
1 large carrot - diced, ¾ cup shelled peas
1 tsp Worcestershire sauce, 2 tbsp tomato puree, 1 tbsp tomato sauce
a few drops Tabasco sauce or ½ tsp red chilli flakes or powder
1½ tsp salt, or to taste

TOPPING

5 large potatoes - boiled, grated and mashed till smooth
4-5 tbsp hot milk, approx., 2-3 tbsp butter
salt & black pepper to taste

1. Heat butter in a pressure cooker. Add the onions and brown slightly. Add the garlic, stir and add the mince. Cook until mince is light brown and the water evaporates, leaving the mince dry.

2. Add the tomato puree, tomato sauce, Worcestershire sauce, salt and chilli flakes or Tabasco sauce. Stir for a few seconds.

3. Add the chopped carrot and peas and stir for a minute.

4. Add ¾ cup water and pressure cook to give 1 whistle, lower heat and cook for 3-4 minutes more. Remove from fire.

5. Drop the pressure by putting the cooker under running water. Remove the lid and return to fire and cook till the excess water evaporates. Check the seasoning and adjust according to taste. Add chopped green chillies if you like.

6. Spread the mince mixture in a baking dish.

7. For the topping, mash the boiled potatoes. Add milk and butter and beat well till soft and smooth. Add enough milk to get a soft consistency. Add salt and pepper to taste.

8. Cover the mince mixture with the potatoes, ripple or score the potato mixture with a fork in a decorative design, by making lines on the potato topping.

9. Preheat oven to 200°C. Bake for 20-30 minutes till the potato topping is golden. Serve hot.

King Edward's Potatoes

Serves 8

6 big potatoes
3 tbsp butter - melted
2 eggs - beaten well
50 gm cheese - grated (½ cup)
1½ tsp salt, or to taste
½ tsp peppercorns - crushed
a pinch of ground nutmeg (*jaiphal*)
1 tbsp tomato sauce

MUSHROOM MIX

200 gm mushrooms - each mushroom sliced into 5-6 pieces
1½ tbsp butter
2-3 garlic flakes - chopped very finely
4 tbsp basil, parsley or coriander - chopped

TOPPING

50 gm cheese - grated (½ cup)

1. Boil the potatoes in salted water until tender. Drain. Peel and grate. Then beat with a wooden spoon until fluffy.
2. Add 3 tbsp of melted butter, beaten eggs, ½ cup grated cheese, salt, pepper, nutmeg and tomato sauce. Beat well to mix well. Set aside.
3. To prepare the mushrooms, melt 2 tbsp butter over a medium-high heat. Add the mushrooms and cook for 4-5 minutes, stirring often, until the liquid evaporates. Stir in the garlic and parsley. Remove from fire.
4. Mix the mushroom mixture into the potato mixture. Check salt and pepper.
5. Spread in a greased, shallow casserole. Cover loosely with foil and bake in a hot oven (400°F/200°C) for 40-45 minutes till golden. Remove foil. Sprinkle with the remaining ½ cup of cheese. Continue baking, uncovered, for 5-7 minutes or more or until the cheese melts and is lightly browned. Serve immediately.

Chicken Roast

Serves 4

1 small chicken (broiler) of 700 gm - cleaned
50 gms butter, 1 tsp thyme, ¾ tsp pepper
1 tsp paprika, ½ tsp salt
4 flakes garlic - chopped finely, 1 tbsp lemon juice

STUFFING

2 onions - sliced and deep fried till golden brown
½ cup grated smoked gouda cheese or cheddar cheese
2 cups chopped spinach, 2 tbsp chopped celery or parsley or coriander
2 tbsp olive oil, 1 tsp finely chopped garlic
½ cup fresh bread cubes (cut bread slice into cubes)
1 tbsp finely chopped pine nuts or almonds, ¼ tsp nutmeg

GLAZE

2 tbsp butter, 1 tsp honey, 1 tsp lemon juice

FOR SAUCE

2 tbsp butter, 1 tsp garlic crushed, 1½ tsp flour, 1½ cups water
1 chicken soup cube, see note on page-21
2-3 tsp HP sauce, few drops tabasco sauce
¼ tsp pepper, a pinch of brown sugar

1. Wash chicken. Pat dry top and cavity of chicken with paper towels. Make 4 light cuts on it. Mix melted butter with thyme, pepper, paprika, salt, garlic, lemon juice. Rub this over and inside the chicken. Cover with cling wrap. Marinate chicken for 1-2 hours or overnight.

2. For the filling, microwave washed spinach for 2 minutes till slightly soft. Discard excess water. Squeeze lightly. Add all other ingredients of the stuffing. Mix well. Stuff in the chicken cavity. Close the cavity with wooden skewers or stitch up with a cotton thread.

3. For glaze, heat butter till it turns brown. Remove from fire and add honey and lemon juice. Brush glaze on the chicken.

4. Wrap the chicken in foil. Place on a greased roasting tray. Roast in a preheated oven for 20 minutes at 190°C/380°F. Then remove foil and bake for 25 minutes, until the chicken is no longer pink when you cut into the thickest part.

5. For sauce, heat 2 tbsp butter in a pan add crushed garlic to it and stir till garlic changes colour. Mix chicken soup cube and flour with 1½ cups water and add to the garlic. Stir till it boils. Add tabasco sauce, HP sauce, sugar and pepper to it. Simmer for 5 minutes. Check seasoning.

6. Place hot roasted chicken in a serving dish. Pour hot sauce over the chicken. Decorate with boiled and sauted vegetables.

Chicken Alexandria

Serves 4

4 small chicken breasts (boneless), each weighing 100-125 gm
(if chicken breast is thick divide it horizontally into two to get 2 pieces of ½" thickness)
1 tbsp lemon juice
2-3 tbsp butter, 150 gm (¾ cup) cream, 1 tsp plain flour (*maida*)
½ tsp salt, ¼ tsp pepper

CHEESE SAUCE
1 tbsp butter, ¾ tbsp plain flour (*maida*), 1 cup milk
2 cubes cheddar cheese - grated, ½ tsp salt and pepper

GARNISH
a few mushrooms - sliced, some chopped parsley
1 cube cheddar cheese - grated

1. Wash chicken pieces and pat dry. Sprinkle lemon juice, salt and pepper. Keep aside for ½ hour.

2. To prepare the cheese sauce, heat 1 tbsp butter. Add the plain flour and stir till it slightly changes colour. Remove from heat and add the milk. Stir well and return to heat. Cook till slightly thick. Add salt, pepper and cheese. Remove from heat.

3. Heat 2-3 tbsp butter in a flat non stick pan. Add the chicken breasts to hot butter and fry on both sides till pale golden, for about 4-5 minutes.

4. Lower heat and add ½ cup water. Cover and cook the chicken breasts till absolutely tender, for about 7-8 minutes.

5. Lift the chicken pieces from the pan. Drain any excess liquid and clean the pan with a paper napkin. (The pan is cleaned so that the chicken residue does not discolour the sauce). Return the chicken pieces to the pan.

6. Mix maida with cream and pour over the chicken pieces in the pan. Stir to coat the pieces well. Cook on low heat for ½ minute.

7. Lift the chicken pieces to a baking dish, leaving behind the cream.

8. Add the cheese sauce to the cream in the pan and blend the cream and cheese sauce. Add ¼ cup of milk to the sauce if it gets too thick.

9. Pour the sauce over the chicken pieces to coat each piece well. Garnish with slices of mushrooms and a little grated cheese.

10. At the time of serving, grill in a preheated oven at 200°C for 5 minutes. Serve with grilled tomatoes and boiled glazed vegetables and steamed rice.

From The Pan

Pan cooked Continental dishes - Pan Fried, Fried and Stews are becoming extremely popular. Food cooked in the pan is tasty and simple.

For cooking chicken in pan, take small tender chicken (broiler). Cook chicken pieces in a flat pan so that they do not overlap each other. Fry the chicken pieces on high heat for the first 5 minutes to brown the chicken as well as to seal the juices. Now lower heat and cook covered for 10 minutes or till chicken turns tender. Over cooking can turn the chicken dry and tasteless. It should remain moist.

For pan frying mutton, use a tenderizer like raw papaya paste to tenderize the meat. Use 1 tbsp of raw papaya paste to 500 gm mutton and keep aside for 2 hours. In the absence of the papaya paste, instead of cooking mutton in the pan, pressure cook mutton to give 2-3 whistles and then keep on low heat for 10 minutes.

Supreme Vegetable Steak

Minced vegetables stuffed with pineapple & cheese, served with creamed spinach.

Serves 2

2 big potatoes - boiled, peeled and grated
1 small carrot - chopped, 5-6 French beans - chopped finely
½ tsp salt, ¼ tsp dry mango powder (*amchoor*)
¼ tsp pepper, ¼ tsp red chilli powder, 1½ tbsp cornflour

FILLING

½ pineapple slice (tinned) - shredded, 1 cube cheese - grated (4 tbsp)
1 tbsp parsley or coriander - chopped finely
4-5 peppercorns - crushed, ¼ tsp salt, or to taste, a pinch of red chilli powder

MUSHROOM SAUCE

1 tbsp butter, 3-4 mushrooms - finely chopped, 1½ tbsp flour (*maida*)
1¼ cups hot water mixed with 1 stock cube (seasoning cube)
½ tsp red chilli powder, ½ tsp white pepper
½ tsp Worcestershire sauce, 1 tbsp tomato puree, 1 tsp tomato sauce, salt to taste

CREAMED SPINACH

1 tbsp butter, ½ tbsp oil, 1 onion - cut into slices, 4-5 flakes garlic - crushed
2 tomatoes - blanched & chopped finely, ½ bundle (250 gm) spinach - chopped
¼ tsp chilli powder, ¼ tsp sugar, ¾ tsp salt and ¼ tsp freshly ground peppercorns
1 tbsp thick cream, ¼ tsp nutmeg (*jaiphal*) - grated

1. Pressure cook carrots and beans in 1/3 cup water to give one whistle. Keep on fire for 2-3 minutes. Remove from fire. After the pressure drops, mash the hot vegetables. If there is any water left in the cooker, mash on fire till the water dries.

2. Mix potatoes, beans-carrots, cornflour, coriander, salt, pepper & red chilli powder.

3. Mix all ingredients of the filling. Make 4 balls of the potato-vegetable mixture. Flatten and stuff ¼ of the filling in each. Form oval shaped steaks and neatly flatten them from the sides. Keep in the refrigerator to chill.

4. To prepare the sauce, heat butter and fry the mushrooms until golden brown. Add the flour and fry on low heat until brown. Remove from heat. Mix the stock cube in hot water and add to the mushrooms. Add tomato puree. Return to fire and cook stirring continuously till thick. Add sauces and salt to taste.

5. To prepare creamed spinach, heat butter and oil. Add onions. Stir for 2 minutes. Add garlic. Stir and add tomatoes. Cook for 5 minutes. Add salt and pepper to taste. Add all other ingredients except cream. Boil and simmer for 4-5 minutes till thick. Add cream and nutmeg. Check salt and pepper. Remove from fire.

6. At the time of serving, heat 5-6 tbsp oil in a non stick pan. Shallow fry steaks on medium heat on both sides till brown and crisp. Drain on paper napkins. Arrange 2 steaks on a serving plate. Top with sauce. Arrange some spinach on the side.

Mince Pattise & Mushroom Sauce

Chicken mince pattise stuffed with herbed cheese, served with mushroom sauce

Serves 3-4

MINCE PATTISE

300 gm chicken mince (*keema*)
½ onion - chopped very finely, 1 tsp ginger-garlic paste
1 slice bread - remove sides and grind in a mixer to get fresh crumbs
1 tsp Worcestershire sauce
1 tsp salt & ¼ tsp pepper to taste

FILLING (HERBED CHEESE)

4-5 tbsp grated mozzarella cheese
½ tsp dried oregano, 1 tbsp finely chopped fresh parsley or coriander

MUSHROOM SAUCE

1 tbsp butter, 3-4 mushrooms - finely chopped, 1½ tbsp flour (*maida*)
1¼ cups hot water mixed with 1 stock cube (seasoning cube), pepper to taste
½ tsp Worcestershire sauce, 1 tbsp tomato puree, 1 tsp tomato ketchup

1. Grind the chicken mince in a mixer for a few seconds to get more binding in the chicken mince. In a bowl, combine chicken mince, onion, ginger-garlic paste, fresh bread crumbs, worcestershire sauce, salt and pepper. Mix well.
2. Mix all ingredients of the filling together. Keep aside.
3. Form 6 balls from the mince mixture. Flatten each ball and put a tbsp of herbed cheese inside. Shape into a ball again and flatten to form 6 pattise. Refrigerate till the time of serving.
4. To prepare the sauce, heat butter and fry the mushrooms until golden brown. Add the flour and fry on low heat until brown. Remove from heat. Mix the stock cube in hot water and add to the mushrooms. Add tomato puree and tomato sauce. Return to fire. Boil. Cook stirring continuously for 3-4 minutes till thick. Add pepper to taste. Remove from fire.
5. To serve, heat ½-1 tbsp oil on low heat in a nonstick pan and coat the bottom of the pan with this oil. Add the pattise. Cook pattise on low heat for about 8-10 minutes. Keep turning sides and pressing the pattise occasionally so that the pattise get cooked from inside and also turn brown on both sides. Transfer to a serving platter. Pour hot mushroom sauce over them. Accompany the pattise with light sesame vegetables, given on page 64 and rice.

Dill Potatoes

Serves 4

4-5 (½ kg) medium size potatoes
1½ tbsp butter
4 flakes garlic - chopped
1 tbsp plain flour (*maida*)
1½ cups (300 ml) milk
4 tbsp (¼ cup) cream
4-5 tbsp (½ cup) fresh dill (green soye leaves) - finely chopped
2 green chillies - finely chopped
½ tsp salt
¼ tsp pepper, or to taste
a few drops of lemon juice
a few spring onion greens

1. Peel the potatoes. Cut them in ¼" thick, round slices.
2. Boil 4-5 cups of water with ½ tsp salt. Add the potato slices to boiling water and boil them till tender but firm. Do not over boil, as it will make the slices soft and break. Drain the potatoes and keep aside.
3. Heat butter in a pan. Add garlic (the butter should not be too hot as the garlic will burn). Stir for a minute and add flour. Cook till light brown. Reduce heat and add the milk, stirring continuously till slightly thick.
4. Reduce heat. Add the chopped dill, chillies, salt, pepper, cream and the boiled potato slices.
5. Stir to coat the potatoes nicely in sauce.
6. Reduce heat. Add a few drops of lemon juice and greens of onion. Remove from fire. Serve hot with garlic bread.

NOTE: Dill is green soya ka saag in hindi language.

Herbed Fish with Tartare Sauce

Serves 4

8 boneless fish pieces, each about 3"
8 fresh white bread slices
¾ cup fresh herbs (thyme, basil or parsley) or 2 tbsp dried herbs & 2 tbsp fresh parsley or coriander
1 tbsp lemon juice, ½ tsp salt
½ tsp white pepper
2 eggs - beaten with a little water

TARTARE SAUCE
½ cup mayonnaise
1 tbsp very finely chopped cucumber, 1 tbsp very finely chopped onion
¼ cup brown vinegar

1. Wash the fish fillet and pat dry on a kitchen towel. Marinate the fillet with salt, pepper and lemon juice. Keep aside for 1 hour in the refrigerator.

2. Trim the sides of the bread and place in a food processor with fresh herbs or dried herbs and parsley. Blend till smooth. Remove and spread the fresh herbed bread crumbs on a plate.

3. Beat the eggs (you can take 2 egg whites only, instead of whole eggs) with 2-3 tbsp water.

4. Heat oil to about ½" height in a pan, on medium heat. Do not make the oil too hot as the fresh bread crumbs will brown very fast before the fish is cooked.

5. Dip the fish fillet in beaten eggs, shake excess egg (this is just done to moisten the fillet) press well onto herbed crumbs. Fry on medium heat till golden brown. Remove on paper napkin and serve hot with tartare sauce.

6. To prepare the tartare sauce, soak the onion and cucumber in vinegar for 10-15 minutes. Strain vegetables from vinegar. Press vegetables gently to remove any excess vinegar. Gently mix them into the mayonnaise. Serve with fish fillets.

Vegetable Sizzler

Serves 2

2 potatoes - boiled & grated, 1 small onion - finely chopped, 1 tbsp butter
1 carrot - chopped, ½ cup peas or 5-6 French beans, chopped
¾ tsp salt or to taste, ¼ tsp dry mango powder (*amchoor*)
¼ tsp pepper, ¼ tsp red chilli powder
1½ tbsp cornflour, 50 gm cottage cheese (*paneer*) - grated
2 slices bread - churned in the mixer to get fresh crumbs

SAUCE

2 tbsp butter, ½ tsp black peppercorns - crushed, 1 tsp garlic - chopped and crushed
1½ tbsp plain flour (*maida*)
4 tbsp tomato puree, 1 tsp Worcester sauce, 1 tsp tomato sauce
½ tsp salt, ½ tsp oregano, ¼ tsp red chilli flakes, 1 cup water

TO SERVE

1 cup pasta - boiled
a few french fries, optional, a few cabbage leaves

1. Pressure cook carrots and beans in 1/3 cup water to give one whistle. Keep on fire for 2-3 minutes. Remove from fire. After the pressure drops, mash the hot vegetables. If there is any water left in the cooker, mash on fire till the water dries.

2. Heat 1 tbsp butter. Add onion and stir till transparent. Add carrots and beans. Add spices. Cook for 2-3 minutes. Mix boiled and grated potatoes. Remove from fire.

3. Add fresh bread crumbs and mix well. Gently mix in the cottage cheese (paneer) and cornflour. Shape mixture into round cutlets of about 2½" diameter. Keep aside in the refrigerator to chill.

4. For sauce, heat 2 tbsp butter in nonstick pan. Add crushed peppercorns. Stir and add garlic. Stir. Add flour. Stir on low flame for ½ minute. Add 1 cup water, tomato puree, Worcestershire sauce, tomato sauce, salt, oregano and red chilli flakes. Cook stirring continuously till a little thick. Remove from fire.

5. For the pasta, heat 1 tbsp butter and add pasta. Saute for a minute. Add 1-2 tbsp of the prepared sauce. Add salt and pepper to taste.

6. Shallow fry the cutlets in oil in a pan till crisp.

7. Remove the iron sizzler plate from the wooden base. Heat the plate by keeping it directly on the flame. Shut off the flame only when the iron plate is really hot.

8. Place 2-3 cabbage leaves on the sizzler plate and spread pasta. Arrange 2 cutlets on it. Pour hot sauce over it. Arrange fries on the side. Dot the iron plate with butter. (When the butter and sauce fall on the hot plate, it sizzles). With the help of a firm pair of tongs (sansi), place on the hot iron plate on the wooden tray. Serve sizzling hot.

Nutty Fish Balls in Tomato Sauce

Serves 6

½ kg fish, preferably boneless - boiled and flaked
2 tsp cornflour, salt and pepper to taste, 2 egg yolks
1 egg white - beaten with 1 tbsp water, ¼ cup cashewnuts - powdered coarsely

SAUCE

3 tbsp oil, 10 flakes garlic - crushed & chopped
1½ cups fresh tomato puree (blend 5 large tomatoes to a puree in a blender)
½ tsp chilli powder, ½ tsp salt, ½ tsp pepper, ½ tsp sugar
1 cup water or fish stock
1 tsp cornflour dissolved in ¼ cup water
1 capsicum - to garnish

1. Boil fish by placing in a covered vessel with ¾ cup water for 10 minutes on low flame after the first boil. Retain stock.
2. Debone and flake the fish, if need be. Mix fish, salt, pepper, cornflour and egg yolks. Make balls with fish mixture.
3. Roll balls first into egg white, then roll over powdered cashewnuts, such that the nuts coat the balls. Fry on medium heat till golden brown. Drain and keep aside.
4. To prepare the sauce, heat 3 tbsp oil, reduce heat and add garlic. Cook till it changes colour. Add tomato puree, cook till thick and oil separates.
5. Add the seasoning, 1 cup water or fish stock. Simmer for 3-4 minutes. Do not add the cornflour paste.
6. At serving time, boil the sauce. Add the cornflour paste, stirring continuously. Cook for 3-4 minutes till thick. Reduce heat. Add the fish balls and heat gently on low heat. Remove from fire. Garnish with fine slices of capsicum. Serve hot.

Aubergines with Sour Cream

An attractive delicious preparation of brinjals.

Serves 8-10

2 longish brinjals of round variety
coriander leaves or boiled peas to garnish

SOUR CREAM
½ cup yogurt - hang for 15 minutes
½ tsp crushed pepper, salt to taste, 1 tsp lemon rind, a few drops lemon juice

SAUCE
1 tbsp oil, 3 large tomatoes - chopped
1 onion - finely chopped, 6-7 flakes garlic - finely chopped
1 jalapeno or green chilli - finely chopped
2 tbsp tomato ketchup, dash of Tabasco sauce
salt to taste, ¼ tsp pepper, ½ tsp red chilli flakes, ½ tsp oregano

1. Cut ¼" to ½" thick rounds of brinjals. Soak in salted water for 15 minutes. Wash and wipe dry with a clean napkin. Heat 3-4 tbsp oil in a non stick pan. Shallow fry the brinjals to a brown colour. Check that they get cooked properly.

2. Hang yogurt for 15 minutes in a thin muslin cloth. Beat hung yogurt with salt and pepper to taste. Grate a lemon gently and add some lemon rind for flavour. Add a few drops of lemon juice too.

3. To prepare the sauce, heat 1 tbsp oil. Add onion and garlic and cook till onions turn soft. Add tomatoes and other ingredients. Cook for 7-8 minutes till thick and dry.

4. Arrange fried brinjals in a micro proof, flat serving plate. Keep aside.

5. At the time of serving, spread the prepared sauce on each piece of brinjal, leaving the edges. Warm in a microwave. Dot with 1 tsp of the prepared sour cream Top with a coriander leaf or a pea and serve immediately.

Chicken Sizzler

Serves 4

MARINATE TOGETHER
2 small chicken breasts, 3 tbsp olive oil, 1 tsp salt, 1 tsp pepper
1 tbsp garlic paste, 2 tsp mustard paste, 2½ tbsp balsamic vinegar

FILLING
4-5 tbsp grated mozzarella, ½ tsp oregano
1 tbsp finely chopped basil or coriander

GINGER ORANGE SAUCE
2 tbsp olive oil, 1 tsp lemon rind, ¼ tsp salt, ¼ tsp pepper
1 tbsp shredded basil
4 tbsp orange tang & 3 tbsp cornflour dissolved in ¼ cup water
½ tbsp lemon juice, 1 tsp ginger juice (finely grate 1 tbsp ginger & squeeze)

TO SERVE
2 cabbage leaves - torn into pieces, a few french fries
3 cups boiled rice mixed with ½ tsp oregano, ½ tsp red chilli flakes
salt to taste and 2 tbsp finely chopped coriander to make coriander rice

1. Wash and pat dry chicken. Slit into half widthwise, keeping one side joint so that the breast opens up like a butterfly. Prick lightly. Mix all ingredients of the marinade. Add chicken to it and rub well to coat the chicken. Keep aside for at least 2-3 hours in the fridge.

2. Put marinated chicken in a pressure cooker with 1 cup water. Allow 2 whistles. Remove from heat and let the pressure drop by itself. When it cools, keep breast aside and use the stock (liquid) for the sauce.

3. For the sauce, heat olive oil. Add the above stock. Bring to a boil. Add orange tang and cornflour dissolved in water, stirring constantly. Cook for a minute only. Remove from fire. Add orange or lemon rind, ginger juice, lemon juice and basil. Add salt pepper if needed.

4. To serve, heat a pan with 1 tbsp oil. Open out the marinated chicken breast and place on the pan. Cook on medium heat, pressing occasionally, for about 1 minute on each side till the chicken is golden. Remove from pan. Sprinkle some cheese, oregano and basil on one side of the hot breast and turn over to cover to make a complete breast.

5. Sprinkle a mixture of 1 tbsp oil and 1 tbsp water on the wooden plate. Keep aside. Heat the iron sizzler plate on high flame. Place a few cabbage leaves on the iron plate. Spread rice on it. Arrange vegetables and french fries on the sides. Place a piece of chicken in the centre. Spoon sauce on the chicken and let it fall on the plate. Place iron plate on the wooden plate to sizzle and make fumes. Serve.

Fettuccine with Chicken

Serves 4

150 gm uncooked fettuccine - boiled (2 large cups)
250 gm boneless chicken - cut into into thin strips
2 tbsp olive oil
2 tbsp finely chopped onion, 150-200 gm mushrooms - chopped
3-4 flakes garlic - crushed & chopped, ½ cup (100 gm) cream
2 tbsp fresh chopped parsley or 1 tsp dry parsley
salt to taste, ½ tsp red chilli flakes, ¼ white pepper
1 tsp oregano

1. Cook the fettuccine in salted boiling water for 10-12 minutes. Drain and rinse under cold water. Keep aside in the strainer for all the water to drain out. Sprinkle 1 tbsp olive oil and toss. Keep aside covered.
2. Heat oil in a pan and add garlic. Stir. Add spring onions and cook for 1 minute.
3. Add the chicken pieces and saute for 2 minutes on high heat till golden. Cover and cook for 1-2 minutes on low heat till tender.
4. Add the mushrooms and stir for 1 minute.
5. Add the cream, reduce heat and simmer for 1-2 minutes till cream reduces.
6. Add parsley, salt, pepper, red chilli flakes and oregano.
7. Add the fettuccine and stir till well coated. Serve at once.

A delicately flavoured stew. Serve with steamed rice or bread.

Serves 8

15 (100 gm) french beans - cut into 1" pieces
3 (150 gm) carrots - cut into small cubes
1½ cups (150 gm) shelled green peas or a few florets broccoli
4-5 florets of cauliflower - cut into medium florets
2 (100 gm) potatoes - cut into ¾" cubes
1-2 bay leaves, 3-4 small onions - each cut into four pieces
3 large onions - sliced
4 tbsp butter
4 cloves (*laung*), 2 sticks cinnamon (*dalchini*)
6-8 peppercorns (*saboot kali mirch*), 2 tbsp plain flour (*maida*)
2 tomatoes - each cut into 8 pieces, 3 tsp Worcestershire sauce
1½ tsp salt, or to taste

1. Slice the large onions.
2. Cut the other vegetables (except green peas) into big pieces.
3. Heat 4 tbsp butter in a big vessel. Add a bay leaf, then add sliced onions and stir fry the sliced onions, for about 4-5 minutes on medium flame, until they turn light brown in colour.
4. Add the cinnamon, cloves and peppercorns and fry for 1 minute.
5. Add the vegetables except tomatoes and fry until light brown.
6. Add 3 cups of water and cook uncovered on low heat, for about 10-12 minutes, until the vegetables and especially the potatoes are done.
7. Mix the flour in ½ cup of water and add to the stew, stirring continuously.
8. After 2 minutes, add the tomatoes, Worcestershire sauce and salt. Cook for 2 minutes. Serve hot.

Serves 8

500 gm mutton (boneless) leg portion - cut in 2" cubes
2 -3 tsp sweet Hungarian paprika
2 onions - chopped finely
1 bay leaf (*tej patta*)
3-4 peppercorns (*saboot kali mirch*)
3-4 flakes garlic - crushed & chopped
5 tbsp oil
2 tbsp flour (*maida*)
2 tomatoes - chopped finely
3 cups hot water mixed with 1 cube chicken super seasoning
1 carrot - cut into round slices or thin long pieces
1 small potato - cut into 8 pieces or 4-5 baby potatoes - boiled or fried
¼ tsp pepper, or to taste
2 tsp cornflour dissolved in ½ cup water

1. Heat oil in a pressure cooker. Add the onions and stir fry till slightly brown.
2. Add mutton, bay leaf, peppercorns and garlic. Stir to mix well. Add paparika. Mix and cook till mutton is brown on all sides, stirring continuously on medium heat for 5 minutes.
3. Add the flour, stir for ½ minute.
4. Add the chopped tomatoes and stir for 2-3 minutes.
5. Add the prepared stock and close the lid of the pressure cooker. Pressure cook to give 3 whistles and lower heat for 15 minutes. Remove from fire. Cool and check for tenderness.
6. Add cornflour paste, stirring continuously. Cook till you get the desired consistency.
7. Add the vegetables and bring to a boil. Simmer for 3-4 minutes till vegetables are slightly tender. Check the seasoning and add paprika, salt and pepper if needed. Serve hot with bread or buttered noodles.

Chicken Stroganoff

Cubed chicken simmered in tomato cream sauce with mushrooms. A little yogurt is added along with the cream, to make the dish lighter.

Serves 4

400 gm boneless chicken (thigh or breast) - cut into 1" cubes
3 tbsp butter
1 small onion - finely chopped
100-150 gm mushrooms - each cut into two pieces
1½ cups chicken stock or water
½ tbsp tomato puree, 1 tbsp tomato ketchup, see note
½ tsp Worcestershire sauce
3-4 flakes garlic - crushed & chopped
1 tbsp flour
¾ cup cream, 2-3 tbsp thick yogurt
½ tsp salt, ¼ tsp pepper and ½ tsp paprika
½ capsicum - chopped into cubes

TO SERVE
garlic bread, page 91

1. Sprinkle salt, pepper and paprika powder over the chicken pieces. Keep aside.
2. Heat a pan with a tight fitting lid or a pressure pan and add 1 tbsp butter. Add the onion and cook till light brown. Add the mushrooms and cook for 1-2 minutes. Remove the mushrooms and onions from the pan.
3. In the same pan add 1 tbsp of butter and add the chicken pieces. Stir fry till well browned on both sides, for about 4-5 minutes. Add 1½ cups of water and close the lid and simmer for 10-12 minutes on low heat till the chicken is tender. If you are using a pressure cooker, give 1 whistle. Lower heat and simmer for 2 minutes. Remove from fire.
4. Take out ½ cup of chicken stock from the chicken in the pan. Cool the stock and blend in the flour and mix well. Keep the flour paste aside.
5. Return the pan with the chicken to heat. Add tomato puree, tomato sauce, garlic and fried onion-mushroom to the chicken in the pan. Add salt, pepper and paprika powder and the blended flour paste. Stir and bring to a boil.
6. Whip cream and yogurt will so that there are no lumps and it becomes smooth.
7. Take the pan off the heat and add cream-yogurt mixture. Blend well. Add chopped capsicum. Heat on very low flame gently and remove just before it starts to boil.
8. Serve with garlic bread as on page 91 or with steamed rice.

NOTE: 3-4 tbsp red wine can be added. In that case there is no need to add tomato puree and ketchup.

Fried Chicken Chasseur

Serves 4

1 small chicken (700 gm) broiler - cut into 4 pieces
3-4 tbsp butter
1 cup chicken stock (200 ml) or 1 chicken stock cube mixed with 1 cup water
2 tomatoes - blanched and pureed
100-150 gm mushrooms - cut into thin slices
2 tbsp tomato ketchup
parsley to garnish
¼ tsp freshly ground pepper

1. Sprinkle salt and pepper on the chicken pieces and keep aside.
2. To blanch tomatoes, boil 1 cup water in a sauce pan. Add the tomatoes and simmer for 2-3 minutes. Drain and peel the skin of the tomatoes. Blend blanched tomatoes to a puree or chop finely.
3. Heat a flat pan with butter. Add the chicken pieces and fry in hot butter for 8-10 minutes on both sides till well browned.
4. Add the stock, tomatoes and sliced mushrooms. Cover and cook gently till the chicken is tender.
5. When the juices have dried and the chicken is tender, add the tomato ketchup.
6. Check the seasoning and sprinkle some salt and pepper to taste. Remove from fire. Garnish with parsley and serve hot with some sesame vegetables given below.

Light Sesame Vegetables

Serves 4-6

250 gm broccoli - cut into small florets
100 gm baby corns - cut diagonally into slices
100 gms mushrooms (small) - keep them whole, only trim the stem
1 carrot - peeled and sliced diagonally
2 tbsp butter or olive oil, 2-3 flakes garlic - crushed
1 tomato - deseeded and very finely chopped
1 tsp salt, ½ tsp pepper, 1 tbsp lemon juice
2 tbsp sesame seeds (*til*)

1. Boil 4-5 cups of water with 2 tsp salt in a pan. Add the vegetables. After the boil returns, keep boiling for ½ minute only. Strain. Refresh in cold water. Keep aside.
2. Heat 2 tbsp butter or oil in a pan. Add garlic. Stir and add the sesame seeds. Stir for a few seconds till golden. Add the blanched vegetables. Cook for 3-4 minutes on medium flame till well coated in butter.
3. Add tomato, salt and pepper. Stir and add lemon juice. Remove from fire. Serve.

Champignons Ala Cream

Mushrooms in a cream sauce.

Serves 6

400 gm small button mushrooms
3-4 tbsp butter
1 tsp dried mixed herbs (basil, thyme, tarragon, sage, oregano), salt & pepper
1 tbsp flour (*maida*)
½ cup milk
¾ cup (150 ml) cream
1 tsp lemon juice
2 tbsp chopped parsley or spring onion greens

1. Wash the mushrooms and pat dry. If small, keep them whole, if large cut into half. Slice the mushrooms. Heat butter in a pan and add the mushrooms and stir fry for 2-3 minutes till light brown.
2. Add 1 tsp of mixed herbs, some salt and freshly ground pepper. Cook for 1-2 minutes to draw out the juices of the mushrooms.
3. Reduce heat. Sprinkle the flour in the pan and stir well. Gradually add milk, stirring continuously. Bring to a boil on low heat.
4. Remove from fire. Pour the cream, lemon and parsley. To serve, warm the mushrooms on low heat and do not let it boil. Serve hot with buttered toasts.

Chicken Italiano

Serves 4

400-450 gm boneless chicken (thigh or breast) - cut into 1" pieces
1 tsp oregano
2 tsp tomato ketchup
½ tsp salt
2 tbsp olive oil

SAUCE WITH VEGETABLES
1 tbsp butter
200 gm mushrooms - each cut into 2 pieces
1 carrot - cut into 1" slices
1½ tbsp plain flour (*maida*)
2 cups chicken stock or 2 cups warm water mixed with 2 chicken seasoning cubes
5-6 tbsp (100 ml) cream

GARNISH
a few black olives, 1-2 tbsp grated cheese, preferably parmesan

1. Marinate the chicken pieces in oregano, ketchup and salt. Keep aside.
2. Heat 1 tbsp butter in a pan and add mushrooms and carrots. Stir fry for 2-3 minutes.
3. Add flour. Stir for 1 minute and add 2 cups stock. Bring to a boil, stirring continuously. Simmer for 2-3 minutes till veggies get cooked.
4. Reduce heat and add cream. Cook on low heat for ½ minute. Remove from fire and keep the sauce aside.
5. Heat 2 tbsp olive oil in a clean pan and add the marinated chicken pieces. Cook stirring, for 4-5 minutes till brown on both sides. Cover and cook for a few minutes till tender. Add the sauce. Bring to a boil on low heat. Remove from fire and serve sprinkled with olives and 1 tbsp parmesan cheese.

Velvety Prawns

Serves 2-3

MARINADE
6-8 large prawns
1 tsp garlic - very finely chopped
1 tbsp parsley - chopped, optional
1 tbsp lemon juice
2 tbsp oil

SAUCE
1 tbsp oil
6-7 flakes garlic - chopped (1 tsp), ¼ of an onion - chopped (2 tbsp)
¼ of a tomato - chopped (2 tbsp), 1 tsp lemon juice
1 egg yolk, ¼ cup cream, ¼ tsp salt and pepper, 1 tbsp chopped parsley

1. Wash and pat dry the prawns. Marinate with garlic, lemon juice and parsley for 5 minutes.
2. Heat 2 tbsp oil in pan. Add the marinated prawns and cook for 1-2 minutes stirring continuously. Remove the prawns in a dish.
3. In the sauce pan add 1 tbsp of oil. Add the onions and garlic and stir till onions turn soft and transparent, for about 1 minute.
4. Add the tomatoes and stir.
5. Add the prawns. Add salt and pepper.
6. Beat cream and egg yolk together. Reduce heat and add the cream-yolk mixture to the prawns. Cook on low flame for 2 minutes till the prawns are well coated in sauce. Add chopped parsley. Serve hot.

Pan Fried Herb Chicken

Serves 4

1 small chicken (650-700 gm) - cut into 4 or 8 pieces
1 tbsp vinegar
½ tsp salt
1½ tsp freshly ground pepper
4 tbsp butter
1 tbsp oil
50-75 gm mushrooms - chopped very finely
1 small onion - chopped very finely
4 tbsp mixed fresh herbs (basil, parsley, mint, coriander) or 1 tbsp mixed dry herbs

1. Wash and pat dry the chicken pieces. Marinate chicken in vinegar, salt and pepper for atleast 2 hours. Keep marinated chicken in the fridge till serving time..

2. To serve, heat 2 tbsp butter and 1 tbsp oil together in a flat non stick pan until foamy. Add the chicken pieces and cook for 5-6 minutes till it turns brown on both sides.

3. Lower heat and add the mushrooms and onions. Stir for 2 minutes. Cover and cook till chicken turns tender, sprinkling a little water if needed.

4. Add herbs and cook for 2 minutes. Add 2 tbsp more butter on the chicken. Remove from fire. Serve hot with boiled mashed potatoes mixed with some melted butter and boiled peas tossed lightly in butter.

Chickpeas with Paneer

Serves 6

100 gms paneer - cut into very tiny cubes
2 cups chick peas (*kabuli channa*) - soaked overnight
¼ of red, yellow or green capsicum, for garnish

WHITE SAUCE
2½ tbsp butter, 1 onion - finely chopped, 2½ tbsp plain flour (*maida*), 2 cups milk
1 tsp salt and ¼ tsp pepper, or to taste, ½ cup grated cheddar cheese (tin or cubes)

TOMATO SAUCE
1 onion - cut into thin slices, ½ kg tomatoes - blended to a puree in a mixer
3 tbsp ready-made tomato puree, 2 tbsp tomato sauce
4 flakes garlic - crushed, ¼ cup basil or coriander leaves
1 tsp dried oregano, ½ tsp chilli powder, ½ tsp sugar, 1 tsp salt, or to taste

1. Drain water from channas. Pressure cook with 4 cups water, 1½ tsp salt to give one whistle. Keep on low heat for about 10 minutes. Remove from fire. Keep aside.

2. To prepare the white sauce, melt the butter in a heavy bottomed pan or a *kadhai*. Add onion and stir till it just changes colour. Sprinkle flour and cook on low heat for 1 minute without browning, stirring throughout. Remove from heat and gradually add the milk. Mix until well blended. Return to heat and cook slowly for about 2 minutes on low heat, stirring throughout until the sauce thickens and coats the spoon well. Remove from fire. Add cheese, salt and pepper. Mix well.

3. For the tomato sauce, heat 2 tbsp oil and fry the onion for 2-3 minutes till it slightly changes colour. Add the fresh tomato puree, ready-made tomato puree, tomato sauce, garlic and basil leaves. Add 1 tsp oregano, ½ tsp chilli powder, ½ tsp sugar and 1 tsp salt. Boil for 10 minutes on low heat till the juice from the tomatoes evaporates and it turns slightly thick. Add the boiled channas along with the water. Cook till the extra water evaporates and the tomato masala coats the channas slightly. Add paneer. Mix. Check salt etc. and remove from fire.

4. In a borosil dish, spread 4 tbsp white sauce at the base. Put channa-paneer in it.

5. Spread the remaining white sauce with a tbsp on channa-paneer, leaving gaps of 2" in between. This way you get red & white strips. Start from the corner, dropping a few tbsp of white sauce in a row, leave a gap & then drop another line of white sauce. Arrange a few coloured capsicum slices diagonally on the white row. Bake in a preheated oven for 20 minutes at 200°C. Serve hot.

Crispy Fried Chicken

Serves 4

4 small chicken breasts (boneless)
½ tsp salt
1 tbsp lemon juice

COATING
½ cup flour (*maida*)
1 tsp salt, ½ tsp black pepper, ½ tsp mustard powder
2 eggs - beaten with a pinch of salt
½ cup dried bread crumbs
2 tbsp chopped coriander
oil for frying

1. Wash the chicken breasts and pat dry. With a sharp knife, divide or split the breast pieces into 2 pieces of ¼" thickness each. (This is done to reduce the thickness of the piece so that they get properly cooked while frying).
2. Beat each piece gently with a mallet or a rolling pin (*belan*). Sprinkle salt and lemon juice and keep aside for 2-3 hours, so that the chicken pieces get tenderized.
3. At serving time, add salt, pepper and mustard to the flour and spread it in a flat plate. Keep the seasoned flour aside.
4. Beat eggs in a bowl with a pinch of salt. Add chopped coriander to the eggs.
5. Spread dried bread crumbs in a flat plate.
6. Heat oil to about ½" height, in a frying pan.
7. Press the chicken piece will into the seasoned flour, dip in beaten eggs, shake off excess egg and press again in bread crumbs.
8. Fry 3-4 pieces at a time on medium heat for 5-6 minutes on both sides till golden brown. Serve hot with mayonnaise and a salad or french fries.

Thin pancakes stuffed with minced lamb.

Serves 8

¾ cup plain flour (*maida*)
2 eggs - beaten well
1 cup milk, 1 tbsp oil
salt & pepper to taste

FILLING

250 gm minced lamb (*keema*)
3 tbsp oil
4-6 flakes garlic - chopped finely
1 onion - chopped finely
2 tsp finely chopped celery, 1 tomato - finely chopped
a few drops Tabasco sauce, ¾ tsp salt, or to taste
1 green chilli - chopped finely, 1 tbsp green coriander - chopped

1. Heat oil in a pressure cooker. Add the onion, garlic and celery. Stir till onions turn golden. Add mince. Cook until mince is light brown and the water evaporates, leaving the mince dry. Add the tomato, salt and chilli flakes or Tabasco sauce. Stir for a few seconds. Add ¾ cup water and pressure cook to give 1 whistle, lower heat and cook for 3-4 minutes more. Remove from fire. Drop the pressure by putting the cooker under running water. Remove the lid and return to fire and cook till the excess water evaporates. Check the seasoning and adjust according to taste. Add chopped green chillies and coriander if you like.

2. For the pancakes, sift flour. Add beaten eggs, milk and oil to make a smooth batter of a thin pouring consistency. Add salt- pepper to taste. Keep aside for 10 minutes.

3. Keep a nonstick pan on medium heat. Rub the bottom of the pan with a little oil. Pour ¼ cup of batter and tilt the pan to roll the batter evenly to cover the bottom of the pan. Cook till set. Do not turn. (Cook on one side only). Remove the pancake on to a plate. Repeat with the remaining batter to make 8 crepes.

4. Take a crepe, keeping the cooked side up. Arrange some filling in a row on one end of the crepe on the cooked side. Fold a little from the opposite sides to enclose the filling and roll upwards tightly. Seal the end with a little flour paste of the crepes. Repeat with all the other crepes. Keep aside. Before serving, heat the non stick pan with 1 tbsp oil. Gently fry the crepes until light brown. Serve with ketchup.

NOTE: Crepes can be made well in advance and shallow fried gently at the time of serving. For chicken crepes, stir fry 1 cup boiled, shredded chicken with ¼ cup shredded cabbage and 1 shredded spring onion to make filling for chicken crepes.

Chicken with Mushroom Cream

Serves 4-5

PAN COOKED CHICKEN

1 chicken (600-700 gm) - cut into 4 or 8 pieces or 500-600 gm boneless chicken
1½ tbsp plain flour (*maida*)
¼ tsp salt, ¼ tsp pepper powder, 1 tsp mustard sauce
3-4 tbsp butter

MUSHROOM CREAM

100-150 gm mushrooms - cut stem into round slices and then cut round into slices
1 tbsp butter, 1 tbsp plain flour (*maida*)
½ cup milk, ¾ cup (150 ml) cream
½ tsp paprika or 1 tsp mustard sauce

1. Wash and pat dry the chicken pieces.
2. Mix flour with salt, pepper and mustard powder. Pat the chicken pieces on the seasoned flour to coat the chicken.
3. Heat 3-4 tbsp butter in a flat non-stick pan. Add chicken pieces in hot butter. Cook on both sides for about 4-5 minutes till light brown.
4. Add ½ cup stock or water. Cover and cook for 5-7 minutes till chicken turns absolutely tender. Remove chicken from heat and keep aside.
5. For the mushroom cream, take a clean pan. Heat 1 tbsp butter and add the mushrooms. Stir for 2-3 minutes till golden. Add a little salt and pepper.
6. Sprinkle flour over the mushrooms and stir to mix well. Add the milk and stir continuously till it boils. Reduce heat and add the cream, paprika or mustard.
7. Add the chicken pieces and cook on low heat till the pieces are well coated with the sauce. Garnish with chopped parsley and serve hot with buttered buns or toasts.

Serves 4-6

½ kg mutton chops (lamb chops)
1 tbsp ginger-garlic paste
2-3 tbsp oil
8-10 small bokchoy or spinach leaves, trimmed
1 potato - boiled, cut into 4 pieces and deep fried

MARINADE

1½ tsp freshly ground black pepper
5-6 tbsp vinegar
1 tsp salt, or to taste
1 tsp Worcestershire sauce
1 tsp soya sauce
5-6 garlic flakes - crushed

1. Wash mutton. Add all the ingredients given under marinade and mix well. Keep aside to marinate for at least 2-3 hours.

2. Heat oil in pressure cooker. Add the ginger-garlic paste, stir fry till it slightly changes colour.

3. Add mutton pieces, leaving the marinade behind. Stir fry for about 10-15 minutes till the juice of mutton gets dried and it turns golden brown. Add the left over marinade and add ¾ cup water. Pressure cook to give 3 whistles. Reduce flame. Keep on low flame for about 10 minutes. Remove from fire. Check for tenderness. If not done, add a little water and keep on low flame for a few minutes. Keep aside till serving time.

4. At serving time, heat the mutton and add bokchoy leaves. Dry the liquid completely. Add big chunks of boiled and fried potatoes. Stir fry for 1 minute. Serve hot.

Serves 2

2 skinless, boneless chicken breast halves
1 tbsp butter, 1 tbsp chopped parsley
1 tsp cornflour
½ tsp mustard powder
½ cup orange juice
2 tbsp orange marmalade
1 tsp soya sauce
a few flaked almonds - toasted, optional

1. Cut each breast into two pieces horizontally. Rinse chicken under cold water, and pat dry with paper towels or a kitchen towel.
2. Melt the butter in a big nonstick pan over medium heat. Cook chicken in butter for about 5 minutes, turning chicken over once with tongs, until golden. Sprinkle a little water and cook covered for about 10 minutes, until juice of chicken is no longer pink when you cut into the centre of the thickest piece. Add parsley and mix well.
3. While the chicken is cooking, mix the cornflour and mustard in a small bowl. Stir in the orange juice, orange marmalade and soy sauce, mixing well.
4. Place the chicken on a serving plate, and cover with aluminium foil or a pan lid to keep it warm. Discard any juices left in the pan and wipe clean the pan with a paper napkin.
5. To make the glaze, pour the orange mixture into the same pan. Heat to boiling over medium heat, stirring constantly. Continue boiling for about 1 minute, stirring constantly, until the sauce is thickened. Add more soya sauce is you prefer a darker colour.
6. Pour the glaze over the chicken on the serving plate. Top with toasted almond flakes.

Serves 4

400 gm cottage cheese (paneer) - cut into 1½"x 2" squares of ¾" thickness

FILLING
½ cube cheese - grated finely (2 tbsp)
6-7 french beans - cut into paper thin slices, ¼ cup finely grated carrot (½ carrot)
¼ tsp salt, ¼ tsp oregano, a pinch of pepper, or to taste
½ tbsp butter, 1 tbsp grated onion (½ onion)

BATTER
3 tbsp plain flour (*maida*), ¼ cup plus 1 tbsp milk
¼ tsp salt, ¼ tsp red chilli flakes, 2 tbsp very finely grated cheese

SALSA
5 tomatoes, 1 onion - chopped finely
2 green chillies - chopped, 2 tbsp chopped coriander, 2 tbsp tomato ketxhup
1 tbsp oil, 1 tsp vinegar, ½ tsp salt and ¼ tsp pepper, or to taste

1. Cut cottage cheese into thick, big rectangular pieces. Divide each piece into 2 pieces. Sprinkle salt & freshly ground pepper on both sides on each piece and keep aside.

2. For the filling, heat butter. Add onion. Stir fry for 2 minutes. Add beans. Cook covered for 3 minutes on low heat till soft. Add carrots, salt, pepper, oregano, grated cheese and stir for 1 minute. Remove from fire and keep aside to cool.

3. Take a piece of cottage cheese. Spread 1 tsp of the filling on it. Press another piece of cottage cheese on it. Turn and press the other side also. Keep aside.

4. For the batter, mix all ingredients of the batter together.

5. For salsa, chop 2 tomatoes and puree the other 3 tomatoes. Heat oil and saute onion and green chillies till onion turns soft. Add all other ingredients and cook for just 1 minute. Do not cook further. Remove from fire. Keep aside.

6. At serving time heat ½ tbsp butter in a pan on medium heat. Dip the stuffed steak in the prepared batter to coat all sides and put in the pan. Cook 4 pieces at a time. Reduce heat after 2 minutes when the edges start changing colour. Turn the side gently with a knife or a flat spoon. Cook till browned on both sides.

7. Serve hot with salsa and sesame vegetables as on page 62.

Serves 4

400-450 gm boneless chicken - cut into 2" pieces
1 tbsp butter
1 bay leaf (*tej patta*)
2-3 cloves (*laung*)
3-4 peppercorns (*saboot kali mirch*)
2½ cups water mixed with 2 chicken super seasoning cubes (stock cubes)

SAUCE

1½ cups milk, approx.
2 tbsp butter
3 tbsp flour (*maida*)
1 carrot - cut into flat chunks
4-5 French beans - cut into 2" pieces
¼ cup shelled peas
salt to taste, ½ tsp crushed pepper
chopped parsley or coriander
2-3 tbsp cream, optional

1. Heat 1 tbsp butter in a pan. Add bay leaf, peppercorns and cloves. Stir fry for a few seconds.
2. Add the chicken pieces. Stir fry for 1-2 minutes.
3. Add the water mixed with stock cubes. Cook on low heat for 15 minutes. You may pressure cook to give 2 whistles and then simmer for 1-2 minutes. Remove from heat.
4. Remove the chicken pieces and strain the stock. Reserve the chicken stock, discard the bay leaf, peppercorns and cloves.
5. For the sauce, mix enough milk, about 1½ cups with the chicken stock to get 4 cups of liquid. Keep aside.
6. Heat 2 tbsp butter in a clean pan. Add flour and stir till light brown. Reduce heat. Add the milk-stock mixture and stirring continuously, bring to a boil.
7. Add the vegetables (carrots, french beans and peas) and cook on low heat for 2-3 minutes.
8. Add the chicken pieces and pepper/salt if needed. Add chopped parsley and cook till you get the desired consistency.
9. Reduce heat and add cream if desired. Remove from heat. Serve hot with slices of bread, buttered and grilled till crisp.

Flavoured Bread Spreads

Put any one of these spreads on slices of garlic bread or any ordinary bread and have it grilled or just as it is! To grill, keep in the oven at 200°C for 12-15 minutes.

Garlic bread - Mix 6-8 crushed flakes of garlic with 6 tbsp softened butter. Add 2 tsp lemon juice and a pinch of salt. Add 2-3 tbsp grated cheese.

Mustard Spread - Mix 2 tsp mustard paste, 1 tsp dried herbs, 1 tsp lemon juice, pinch of salt & pepper with 6 tbsp softened butter. Add 2 tbsp grated cheese if you like.

Coriander Cumin Spread - Mix 1 tbsp finely chopped fresh coriander, 1 tsp lemon juice, 1 tsp coarsely ground cumin, salt and black pepper with 6 tbsp softened butter.

Herb & Mushroom Spread - Mix 2 tsp dried herbs, 1 cube grated cheddar cheese, 2-3 finely chopped mushrooms together. Blend herbs, cheese and mushrooms in a blender to a paste. Mix this paste with 6 tbsp softened butter and use.

Baked Bread Loaf

Serves 8

1 French loaf

LEMON FLAVOURED BUTTER
6 tbsp butter - softened, rind of ½ lemon, 1 tbsp lemon juice
a pinch salt, ¼ tsp freshly ground black peppercorns

1. Slit the loaf into ½" thick slices, leaving the loaf attached at the bottom.
2. To prepare the lemon spread, mix butter with lemon rind, juice, salt and pepper.
3. Spread the butter inside each slit and little over the top.
4. Wrap the loaf in an aluminium foil and keep aside.
5. To serve, bake in a preheated oven at 200°C for 15-20 minutes.
6. Open the foil for the last 5 minutes to make the top crisp.

Desserts & Puddings

Blueberry Cheese Cake

Serves 8

BASE
1½ packets (15) good day biscuits
5 tbsp melted butter, a loose bottom cake tin of 8" diameter

CHEESE CAKE
400 gm cream
½ cup powdered sugar, or to taste, 4 tbsp level cheese spread
4 tbsp blue berry jam - beat till smooth
3½ tsp gelatine

TOPPING
½ cup blueberry topping OR
4 tbsp blue berry jam, mixed with ½ cup grape juice and 2 tsp cornflour

1. Crush biscuits to a coarse powder in a mixer.
2. Add melted butter and mix well. Press into the cake tin. Keep to chill while making the cheese cake.
3. Sprinkle gelatine in ¼ cup water in a small pan. Let it stand for 5 minutes. Keep on low heat, stirring, till it dissolves. Do not let it boil. Keep aside.
4. Beat cheese spread with sugar till smooth. Add jam and mix well.
5. Beat cream till fluffy. Add cream to the cheese spread mix. Beat again nicely.
6. Add gelatine solution in small quantity, mixing well each time quickly with the other hand. Pour mixture on the biscuit crust. Chill till set.
7. Spread the ready made blueberry topping. Alternately, cook jam with water and cornflour for 2-3 minutes till a thick topping is ready. Cool and pour over the cake. Chill well before removing from the tin.

Serves 6

3 cups milk
9 tsp sugar
3 tbsp milk powder
1 tsp vanilla custard powder
3 eggs
1 tsp vanilla essence

CARAMEL TOPPING
4 tsp sugar

1. Mix the milk with sugar, milk powder and custard powder. Mix well to dissolve all the lumps. Keep it on fire and boil stirring continuously. After the boil, reduce heat and simmer for 5 minutes. Remove from heat and cool.
2. Beat the eggs and vanilla essence well with an electric hand beater till light and fluffy.
3. Add the well beaten eggs to the cooled milk mixture. Mix well but do not beat too much. Keep aside.
4. Sprinkle 4 tsp of sugar at the bottom of a jelly mould. Place the mould over a slow flame holding it with a tongs and melt the sugar till the liquid turns golden brown. Remove from fire and spread it evenly over the base and sides of the mould. Cool till the sugar is set at the bottom and sides of the vessel.
5. Pour the milk-egg mixture in the mould. Cover well with aluminium foil and place a lid on top.
6. Pour 1½ cups water in a pressure cooker. Place the covered mould in it. Pressure cook to give 4 whistles. Remove from heat. Let the pressure drop by itself.
7. Keep the pudding in the fridge so that it gets cold and sets well. Do not unmould till it turns cold.
8. To unmould at the time of serving, run a knife all around the mould and then invert it on a plate. Give a slight jerk to the mould to take out the pudding.

NOTE: This pudding can be baked in small individual ovenproof bowls at 200°C for 15 minutes. Cover the bowls with foil before putting them in the oven and bake in a water bath (bain marie). To make a water bath, fill a baking tray with 1" water and place pudding bowls in it. Bake in the oven as given.

A delicious dessert for a summer dinner. So refreshingly different!

Serves 8

400 gm (2 cups) cream
3 lemons (6 tbsp lemon juice)
4 large eggs
a few drops of lemon yellow colour
1 cup powdered sugar, or to taste
½ tsp vanilla essence
4 tsp gelatine, ¼ cup water

DECORATION

a few glace cherries, lemon twists,
10-12 almonds - crushed roughly

1. Prepare a souffle dish by tying around it a double band of aluminium foil with its fold at the bottom so that it stands about 2" above the top of the dish. If you wish you can secure the foil with salo tape instead of a thread.
2. Extract the juice of all lemons, keep aside.
3. Separate the egg yolk and white of the eggs.
4. Beat egg yolks in a steel bowl with the lemon juice and sugar.
5. Boil a large pan of water. Remove water from fire. Place the bowl of egg yolk-sugar mixture in hot water and beat with a n electric hand beater or whisk until creamy. Remove from hot water and beat until cold. Keep aside.
6. Add gelatine to ¼ cup water kept in a small pan. Dissolve gelatine on low heat.
7. Add gelatine solution to the egg yolk mixture gradually and stir well. Allow it to set a little in the refrigerator. Do not let it become too stiff or set. (Make quite certain the egg yolk-gelatine mixture has stiffened only slightly before adding the cream and egg whites. If it oversets, i.e. solidifies even a little, keep it over a pan of hot water and stir till it is semi-liquid again).
8. In the meanwhile whip cream with vanilla essence till it becomes thick and attains a soft peak stage. Keeping aside ¼ cup (50 gm) whipped cream for decoration, fold in rest of the whipped cream, into the semi-liquid egg yolk mixture.
9. Beat egg whites with colour till stiff peaks are formed. Fold in stiffened egg whites.
10. Pour into the prepared souffle dish, refrigerate until set; then gently remove the paper.
11. To decorate, gently stick the almonds on the sides above the dish. Whip the left over cream (¼ cup) till stiff peaks are formed and the peaks can hold their shape. Put the cream in an icing bag. Chill for 10 minutes and then decorate the souffle with whipped cream, lemon twists and glace cherries.

Devil's Chocolate Temptation

Serves 8

COCOA DEVIL'S CAKE
1 cup ordinary sugar, 1¼ cups powdered sugar
½ cup cocoa powder, 1 cup curd
¾ cups (90 gm) oil, 2 cups (200 gm) plain flour (*maida*)
2 large eggs, 1 tsp soda-bi-carb, 1 tsp vanilla essence

TO SOAK
¾ cup cold milk, 1 tbsp sugar, 1 tsp rum or brandy (optional)

CHOCOLATE CREAM FILLING
200 gm whipping cream (1 cup), 4 tbsp powdered sugar
3-4 tbsp cocoa mixed with 3-4 tbsp cream to get a smooth paste, ½ tsp vanilla essence

TRUFFLE TOPPING
100 gm fresh cream, 1 tsp butter - softened, 150 gm cooking chocolate - chopped

1. To prepare the cake, mix 1 cup ordinary sugar, curd, vanilla essence and cocoa in a large pan. Beat well till sugar dissolves and is well blended. Keep aside. Beat powdered sugar and eggs till frothy and double in volume. Add oil to the eggs gradually, beating all the time. Sift flour and soda-bi-carb together. Add ½ the flour and ½ the beaten eggs to the cocoa mixture in the pan. Mix well. Add the left over flour and eggs and beat well till the mixture is smooth.

2. Bake in the prepared tin at 180°C for 1 hour. Remove from oven. Cool. Remove from tin. Cut into 3 pieces. Mix ¼ cup of cold milk with 1 tbsp sugar & 1 tsp rum or brandy. Soak each piece of cake with 3 tbsp of this milk. Keep aside to cool.

3. For the filling, beat cream with powdered sugar, cocoa paste and essence till soft peaks form. Beat further very carefully with a spoon till stiff peaks are ready.

4. Place a piece of cake on a serving plate. Soak cake with ¼ cup prepared milk. Spread half of the chocolate cream on it. Invert the second piece of cake on it. Soak again.

5. Spread the left over cream. Finally place the last piece of cake on it. Soak lightly. Press very lightly. Dust the top to get rid of any crumbs. Keep aside.

6. For the truffle topping, heat the cream in a small heavy bottomed pan, on low heat (do not boil). Add chocolate pieces and butter and heat stirring continuously, till chocolate melts and you get a smooth paste. Remove from fire and let it cool to room temperature. Immediately pour over the cake. Serve topped with fresh fruit if you like.

Prune & Walnut Pie

Prunes & walnuts are baked on a short crust pastry shell. A loose bottomed flan tin of 9" diameter is ideal for making it.

Serves 10

SHORT CRUST PASTRY
200 gms (2 cups) flour (*maida*)
¼ cup semolina (*suji*)
a pinch of baking powder
110 gms salted butter (cold and solid)
3 tbsp powder sugar
1-2 tbsp ice cold water to bind

FILLING
100 gm prunes - stoned and chopped finely, 4 tbsp chopped walnuts
4 apples - peeled and grated
½ cup water
2 tbsp lemon juice
6 tbsp honey, 2 tbsp sugar or to taste

1. For the short crust pastry, cut cold butter into tiny cubes.
2. Sift flour with baking powder. In a blender put the flour and semolina. Add the butter and churn for a few seconds. Scrape the sides with a spatula or a knife and churn again for a few seconds only. Do not churn the mixer too much. Transfer to a mixing bowl and mix lightly.
3. Add just enough ice cold water to form a dough. Wrap in a damp cloth and keep in the fridge for 15-20 minutes to get cold.
4. For the filling, mix all ingredients except walnuts and prunes. Heat on slow fire, for about 10 minutes, till pulpy and almost dry. Check sweetness and add more sugar if required. Add walnuts and prunes, keeping aside a few for the topping. Remove from fire and keep aside.
5. To make the pie, keeping aside a lemon sized ball of dough, roll out the rest of the pastry between two plastic sheets, so that it is ¼" thick and 4" bigger in diameter than the flan tin or the pie dish, such that it covers the base & the sides of the tin or pie dish. If you find it difficult to roll it, place the dough in the tin and spread it out to cover the bottom and the sides.
6. Prick the base lightly with a fork. Bake at 200°C in a preheated oven for 16-18 minutes or till the pastry shell turns light brown. Remove from oven.
7. Arrange the dry filling over it. Level it. Roll out the remaining dough and cut strips. Arrange strips on the pie and brush with honey. Arrange some prunes on top if you like. Keep aside till serving time. At the time of serving, bake for 10-12 minutes in a preheated oven at 150°C. Serve hot with vanilla ice cream or fresh cream.

It can be made with chocolate or with cocoa powder. Add extra sugar if cocoa is used.

Serves 8

80 gm cooking chocolate or 3 tbsp cocoa mixed with 6 tbsp water
3 eggs, 1 tbsp gelatine
1½ tsp instant coffee powder, 3 tbsp powdered sugar, or to taste
1½ cups (300 gm) cream - whipped till fluffy, 2 tsp rum or brandy (optional)

1. Chop chocolate roughly, put in a saucepan. Heat 2 cups water in a smaller sauce pan and stir the chocolate over hot water, without touching the water, until melted (double boiler). Or, make a paste of cocoa with water and cook in a double boiler till well-blended. Add coffee powder and mix well. Remove from heat, cool a little.
2. Add gelatine to ¼ cup water kept in a small pan. Heat on low flame till it dissolves.
3. Separate the eggs, blend in egg yolk and sugar into the cooled chocolate mixture. Beat until mixture is smooth and thick. If using cocoa add 4 extra spoons of sugar, i.e. 7 tbsp sugar. (For making mousse with chocolate, 3 tbsp sugar is enough.)
4. Add gelatine, stirring continuously.
5. Beat chilled cream till slightly thick and fluffy. When the chocolate mixture becomes quite cool, fold in whipped cream and brandy.
6. Beat eggs whites stiffly and fold gently into the mixture. Spoon into thin stemmed glasses for individual serving or in a glass dish. Refrigerate until firm. Serve topped with cherries and mint.